THE LOVE OF GOD

*A Startling Revelation of
Paul's Letter to the Ephesians*

www.ingramcontent.com/pod-product-compliance
Lightning Source LLC
Chambersburg PA
CBHW072014040426
42447CB00009B/1627

TABLE OF CONTENTS

INTRODUCTION

Background of the City and Church at Ephesus

Ephesus was the center or headquarters of the temple and worship of the Roman goddess Diana (also known as Artemis in Greek mythology). A temple was built there in her honor in 550 BC eventually being counted as one of the original Seven Wonders of the Ancient World. It was claimed to be the largest structure in the world at the time. In addition the temple was believed to be built by 'Ephesus', the son of a river god and Diana's statue is said to have fallen from Jupiter. So the pagan culture was well established before the Apostle Paul arrived. Some of his ministry and opposition there is recorded in Acts chapters 18 and 19.

The population at the time was between 30-50,000 making it the third largest city in Asia (Asia Minor or present day Turkey). For hundreds of years Ephesus was ruled by various despots and kings motivated by taxation and control. When Augustus rose to power in Rome in 27 BC he made Ephesus the capital of Western Asia Minor. The city finally began to flourish in commerce and as a seat of Roman government. Some historians placed it in importance and size second only to Rome.

Such was the setting when Paul and others brought the Gospel to Ephesus. All was relatively peaceful (compared to other stops on Paul's itinerary) until the silversmiths saw their sales of 'Diana' idols diminish. Fearing a continued loss of revenue they banded together and brought Paul and his friends before the mob they had stirred up. After some hours of shouting and disputing, the town clerk dismissed the assembly and the accused were released unharmed. The Apostle left for Macedonia shortly thereafter and only returned briefly some years later to visit and encourage his son in the faith, Timothy. As far as we know Timothy continued permanently in his ministry as Pastor to the church at Ephesus.

Paul deeply loved Timothy and the church where he left him in charge. His emotional final visit to Ephesus is recorded in Acts 20:17-38.

Background of the Letter to Ephesus

Paul wrote of church order and structure to the Corinthians and to Titus. And his heart for the church under the care of his beloved son in the faith can be found in First and Second Timothy. But the Apostle Paul's letter to the church at Ephesus is his least personal and most lofty—and possibly intended for all the churches in the area similar to Galatians.

Ephesians is the first recorded of the 'Prison Epistles'. These consist of Ephesians, Philippians, Colossians and Philemon. They were written around 64 AD from Rome while Paul was imprisoned under house arrest. While there he ministered to a number of the Roman population and to those of the Roman church as well as to many guards and those of Cesar's court.

He certainly considered the fact that he may never see these churches again. Indeed he never did see the church at Colosse (or Laodicea). So his tone is eternal, but not melancholy. His final letter (that we know of) was written only a few years later to Timothy. Here Paul is looking beyond the earthly trials we may endure. But he does not say that our blessings must wait until we pass into heaven.

He begins with assuring those in Ephesus (and us) that we are already blessed with every spiritual blessing in Christ (1:3). He goes on in increasingly lofty terms to detail our heavenly existence and experience here in this time, on this earth.

Such is this message entitled "The Love of God".

"But God, who is _rich in mercy, for his great love wherewith he loved us_, Even when we were dead in sins, hath quickened us together with Christ, (by grace ye are saved;) And hath raised us up together, and made us sit together in heavenly places in

Christ Jesus: That in the ages to come he might <u>show the</u>
<u>*exceeding riches of his grace in his kindness toward us*</u> *through*
Christ Jesus" (Ephesians 2:4-7 KJV).

In chapters 1-3 the Spirit through the Apostle defines that love (if earthly language were even adequate). And then in chapters 4-6 He describes how to use (walk in) that love—in the church and in our families—and then how that love equips us to stand against and defeat the enemy of our souls.

This God by His Spirit and through His Son has gone to lengths beyond our imagination in our behalf to show His love for us. And this revelation of that love by the hand of His Apostle is penned in such supernatural language that if you will let it, will take you to the very throne room of God.

But why a book about God's Love from the point of view of Paul's letter to the Ephesians? Wouldn't First John or the thirteenth chapter of First Corinthians be more appropriate?

Well it would certainly be more familiar. But...di*d you know that only two books in all of scripture mention 'love' more often (for their size) than Ephesians. Only First John and the Song of Solomon mention 'love' more per chapter. And Solomon's treatise is about marital love and only reflects the love of God allegorically. In contrast, Ephesians speaks very specifically of God's 'love' and uses the term fully twice as many times (total) as the first four books of the Bible combined.*

Most (including me) would agree that a basic study of the love of God would by default include the Apostle John's writings. But while reading (again) the first chapter of Ephesians I believe I heard God's Spirit say plainly, "I want you to meditate this chapter until you receive the, *"spirit of wisdom and revelation"* that I spoke of there."

I did as He said. And what came of it was an overwhelming revelation of the grace and goodness of God. He actually <u>wants us to know what His love did for us</u>.

"...having the eyes of your heart flooded with light so that you can know and understand the hope to which He has called you, and how rich is His glorious inheritance in the saints...And so that you can know and understand what is the immeasurable and limitless and surpassing greatness of His power in and for us who believe as demonstrated in His mighty strength which He exerted in Christ when He raised Him from the dead..." (AMP)

In other words, He's not holding anything back. It is as if He waited so long to regain His beloved family that He is almost beyond expression of His great love. He has tried to explain His position many times but none better than the 'Lovesick Father' in Luke chapter fifteen. We know the story by what we in our sin-conscious condition call the 'Prodigal Son'. But focus on the Father. He has no communication as to his son's whereabouts or well being. And he watches daily the empty horizon ...hoping. Make no mistake. He did not just spot his son's return the day he came back by chance. His heart was in his hand daily as he yearned for the safe return of his beloved son.

That is the Father's message through Jesus as amplified in the first chapter of Ephesians.

After meditating that first chapter for some time I made copious notes on what I expected to be about wisdom and revelation. What happened next however is that I could not stop meditating and researching this heavenly book. Several weeks later I had penned my thoughts and the Holy Spirit's revelation of all six chapters.

I discovered much about wisdom and revelation. But the underlying theme is that God by His Spirit is desperate for us to know how boundless and extravagant is His love for us.

My prayer for you is the same as Paul's. *That the God of our Lord Jesus Christ, the Father of glory may give unto you the spirit of wisdom and revelation in the knowledge of Him*...and who is '*Him*'?According to the Holy Spirit by the Apostle John, His Name is 'Love'.
1 John 4:7-10.

The Love of God is for you. You may be familiar with the scripture from the gospel of John: "*For God so loved the world that He gave His only begotten Son, that <u>whoever</u> believes in Him should not perish but have everlasting life.*" His Love truly is for all. But the receiving of it is our part. All of the promises of God in this book and indeed in His Book are for those who will receive. Church attendance and good deeds are good ideas but not counted in 'receiving'. So if you have never 'received' (Jesus calls in being born again or born from above) then pray this prayer from your heart and you will become one of the '*whoevers*' mentioned in that verse above. Eternity is a very long time. Don't leave it to chance.

God, you know me better than I know myself. You know that I have fallen short of Your righteousness. We all have. But You paid the price of Yourself that I might be set free.

I confess and turn from sin with Your help and I receive Your gift of salvation by faith now. I believe in my heart and confess with my mouth that God raised Jesus from the dead. I am saved, healed, delivered and born from above. I am a child of God and Joint Heir with Jesus Christ. You are now truly my Father and I commit the rest of my life...and beyond...to Your care in Jesus' name. Now, baptize me, Father in your powerful Holy Spirit and bless me with a prayer language that I might commune with You on a level beyond my own understanding. I pray and receive all by faith in Jesus' name. Thank You for Your unspeakable gift. Amen.

Now find a good Bible believing / preaching church and get involved. And email us for some free information to help as well as answer some questions you may have. Our contact information **Info@Axxiom.org** is also on inside of the cover. *And welcome to the family!*

THE LOVE OF GOD

A Heavenly Revelation of
Paul's Letter to the Ephesians

CHAPTER ONE
GOD'S PRAYER FOR US

[1] Paul, an apostle of Jesus Christ by the will of God, To the saints who are in Ephesus, and faithful in Christ Jesus: [2] Grace to you and peace from God our Father and the Lord Jesus Christ. [3] Blessed [be] the God and Father of our Lord Jesus Christ, who has blessed us with every spiritual blessing in the heavenly [places] in Christ, [4] just as He chose us in Him before the foundation of the world, that we should be holy and without blame before Him in love,
[Ephesians 1:1-4 NKJV]

Paul begins this revelation of heaven's view of salvation[1] bestowing on us grace and peace and blessing. Not just a salutation or customary greeting; he is speaking from the Spirit of the Living Almighty LORD of Heaven blessing His creation with all that He has.

A Kingly offering to those who have chosen to be His subjects; and whom He has chosen to love, cherish, adopt and bestow His very best.

And that is what this book is about. We are going to look at God's Love shed abroad in our hearts[2] by His grace like you've never seen it before. God's Love is nothing new. And God's grace is almost colloquial. But these terms are

---

[1] Heaven's view of salvation can be seen in the Hebrew 'yeshivah' translated 'salvation'. It means welfare, prosperity, deliverance and victory. The Greek, 'soteria' means deliverance, preservation, salvation and health, redeemed from all earthly ills.

[2] Romans 5:5 (KJV)

like many others in God's Word that become so familiar in our conversation and experience that they lose their impact.

What we call 'revelation' for instance is the ability of God's Word by His Spirit to startle us. Doctrines don't startle. Creeds don't startle. Hymns or even contemporary Christian lyrics don't startle. Often even God's Word becomes commonplace and while our spirit says, *"Amen"* our flesh is yawning. But a new revelation of John 3:16 may very well startle you.

> *Having lost all He had, He gave all that He had left.*

This short verse was just a part of Jesus' revelation to Nicodemus (and to us) of the Father's heart. A Father who had lost everything— His beloved family, His creation, His dream of innumerable offspring with whom He could share His very life and heart of Love. What made it worse was that His beloved son's treason caused a separation that even He could not violate. Walking with Adam in the cool of the day was His purpose--fellowship and relationship at its best.

But that all ended one day when spiritual death infected the first son of God (the first Adam).

By connecting to his new god, satan[3] he disconnected from His true Father, shutting Him out and making himself incapable of standing in His presence.[4]

The Father's appearance from then on to those whom He addressed was by voice only or with the hearer sufficiently protected (as Moses[5]). The glory of God which

---

[3] Though technically a proper noun and therefore subject to capitalization, I have taken license to refuse this honor to the sworn enemy of our souls. In addition I have aligned myself with those who honor the Creator by capitalizing personal pronouns referring to Deity...at the risk of being grammatically incorrect but without apology.

[4] And not because God refused him. God's glory, while not mentioned by name until many chapters later, is described as Light. And that Light is a consuming fire. In the face of Light darkness is destroyed. So God was forced to send Adam and Eve away and never appeared to His fallen creation again.

[5] Exodus 33:18-23

Adam possessed until separated from the source of that Glory would have consumed him.

God's glory is unapproachable by human flesh. Unredeemed man cannot stand in the presence of God's perfection; which explains why Jesus did not come to reform us or to be a good example. In our spiritually dead state (separated from God) our goodness or 'righteousness' is obliterated by His glory.[6]

So, continuing with our revelation.

His plan from the beginning was to enjoy eternity with you.

Unable to touch, hug or even come near His chosen and beloved family, God waits. And finally it is time. Having lost all He had, He gave all that He had left: His own Son from eternity as the final and ultimate price (sacrifice) to regain or redeem all that He lost. Or as Scripture puts it, *"...when the fullness of the time was come, God sent forth his Son, made of a woman, made under the law,*[7] Untainted by Adam's seed, *this* Son of God was qualified to be the perfect sacrifice (Lamb of God) to redeem God's lost family.

Of course you know all that, but the revelation is seeing it all from the Father's point of view. His desperate love led Him to give up all He possessed to gain...*you*.

We talk about spending eternity with God (which is glorious beyond description) but His plan from the beginning was to enjoy spending eternity with *you*.

Have you ever thought about that? God so loved the world (His family) that He *gave*...He already had Jesus. But He wanted more to love. And when that attempt failed, He gave all He had left to regain what was lost.

---

[6] But we are all as an unclean thing, and all our righteousnesses are as filthy rags; and we all do fade as a leaf; and our iniquities, like the wind, have taken us away. Isaiah 64:6

[7] Galatians 4:4

That is the Love of God.

Now let's go from there and see if you and I can handle even more revelation of God's startling and limitless Love.

Certainly you would agree that what we call salvation is more than enough. But the God who is Love and whose expression of that grace is beyond imagining is pleased to go beyond all that we can ask or even think. This "grace" is the unmerited favor of God. Or one definition that goes beyond any other I've heard is, *"God's overwhelming desire to treat you and me (His family) as if sin never existed."* [8]

> **God's overwhelming desire is to treat you and me as if sin never existed.**

"As if sin never existed". We know it did (does) exist of course. But did you know that He does not. If you could measure the distance from East to West then you could begin to see how far away He has put sin from Him. In another place He has simply forgotten. [9]

That's Grace. But the only hindrance to God's goal of treating us as if sin never existed is our consciousness of it. It's true. We think about it all the time. I don't mean we think about committing it all the time. [10]

I am not talking about 'sinning'. I am talking about the past. I am talking about what is already forgiven. Retaining a consciousness of all that has ever gone wrong is not humility. It is disobedience.

John in his first epistle makes it clear that forgiveness is readily available for sin. [11] And furthermore He does not stop at forgiveness. He is faithful and just not only to forgive

---

[8] Kenneth Copeland, KCM.org

[9] Psalm 103:12; Jeremiah 31:34; Hebrews 10:17

[10] If that is the case then you need to get busy confessing and receiving your cleansing from all unrighteousness..Or maybe you just need to get saved and be made God's righteousness in Christ (see page 14).

[11] Just for the asking. Confess it. And don't wait. God already knows about it. He just wants you to get rid of it. And the penalty? Jesus already paid it. 1 John 1:9

16

but to cleanse. What does that mean? That means your sin is washed away. Gone. Lost forever. Cast into the sea of forgetfulness (Micah 7:19). And if you are cleansed from all unrighteousness then what's left?

That's right. Righteousness. In fact you are made the very righteousness of God in Christ...which by the way you became the instant you were born again. Read 2 Corinthians 5:17-21 and Romans 3:21-22. The only challenge to the process is *our receiving*—a common problem throughout scripture...and in our lives.

Paul quotes Jesus as saying, "It is more blessed to give than to receive[12]." But for us who have been redeemed by the unfathomable love of God, it is sometimes much more difficult to receive than it is to give. Think about it. We enjoy gifts and surprises. But when it is more than expected, we say, *"You didn't have to do that."* or *"I couldn't possibly accept this."* Of course you didn't have to do that...*that's why it's called a gift!*

Our ego and natural man is much more comfortable giving. Believe it or not it does our self image (or ego) good to give. This also is not humility but pride.[13]

God built 'receiving' into His economy. But religion[14] (tradition) has also built into it much that we can do to assuage our pride and satisfy our flesh that wants the supremacy. Grace can do that to people. The Apostle Paul had constant problems with those who wanted to add to Christ's free gift purchased at the cross. To those who had

---

[12] Acts 20:35

[13] Giving out of obedience (to God's Word) takes humility. Giving to satisfy our own agenda is pride.

[14] 'Religion' has many definitions. It is seldom mentioned in scripture and usually in the negative. The most religious folks in the Gospels were the Priests, Pharisees, Sadducees and Scribes...none of which got along with Jesus very well. When I use 'religion' I am referring to the organized traditions that have accumulated over the years (centuries) that according to Jesus make the Word of God of no effect. See Mark 7:6-13

trouble receiving without mixing their own works he said, "...
[for you, then] Christ is dead in vain."[15]

Receiving without some qualifying and commensurate pay-back on our part makes our flesh feel subservient. Wanting to repay (or at least 'work for') what we have received from God is not dissimilar to our natural reluctance to receiving a return on our giving.

> **Before anyone knew what 'political (or religious) correctness' even meant.**

If we can just get past the feelings and resistance of our flesh then we will see the benefit to God's Kingdom of that return. It's not just to bless us. When we give it puts us in a position of God's trust. Did you know He is looking for those He can trust? It's true. If He knows we can be trusted with His resources then He naturally wants to funnel more our way.[16] Therefore the return is so that we can bless others even more. Some simple math and Biblical logic here will reveal God's Kingdom economy and His plan to exponentially bless His people and all the nations (families) of the earth...and provide seed for future provision.[17]

If we say we don't expect or need the return He has established for that purpose then we are saying, *"I've got a good income. Let someone else who really needs it believe for a return on his giving."* In other words, *"I can handle this."* And the orphanage in Uganda in need of $20,000 for medical supplies, staff and expansion waits for Bill Gates to be in need of a tax deduction...or for UNICEF to help along

---

[15] Galatians 2:20-21

[16] Our usual response to this is, "Well, I surely don't give in order to get. I have a higher view of 'giving' than to cheapen it by expecting a return." If that were really the case then I expect you have based that view on scripture. The only problem is that it's not in there. Every offering from Genesis to Revelation God said He would bless and return even more. And He's the same way. He gave the offering of His Son that He would receive "...many sons unto glory." Hebrews 2:9-10.

[17] Genesis 18:18; 22:18; 26:4. In fact in Galatians 3:8 He calls that promise, "the Gospel"! See also 2 Corinthians 9:10.

with their godless and humanistic strings attached. When will we learn that this is God's plan for the church?

Religion takes advantage of this twist in our nature and gives us "Seven steps to God" or "Do this and you will be forgiven" or "You're forgiven but now you must get serious about your devotions and prayer life" or "God helps those who help themselves".

Noah Webster's 1828 dictionary gives one definition of 'religion' as 'bondage'. I refer to this particular version because he uses scripture to validate and expand his definitions. And it was published before anyone knew what 'political (or religious) correctness' even meant.

> *'Peace' is His overwhelming desire to see us enter into His rest.*

Yes, the truth is that if we could escape the bondage of religion and rid our consciousness of any remembrance of sin (or thoughts of redeeming ourselves) then the presence and power and anointing and love of God's Holy Spirit would have free reign in our lives. Where do I get that from? Read Hebrews chapters nine and ten; especially 9:14 and 10:2 for starters. Then look up 'boldness' and 'boldly' and 'access' and 'confidence' in your concordance. The results will bless and inspire you.

So receive the grace (favor / love) of God. He longs for you to receive (without the usual, *"Oh you shouldn't have"*) and come boldly into His presence[18] as the son or daughter He yearns to love and to bestow His very best.

Next we are to receive 'Peace'.

---

[18] Did you notice the change. After the fall God's beloved family had to leave His presence or be consumed. Now having been made the righteousness of God in Christ we can come *boldly* before His presence. This is currently limited to our re-created spirit. Our redeemed bodies are yet future but the real you *is* your spirit. Come boldly today.

Everything that has just been said about grace applies to God's willingness to give us His peace. And if 'grace' is His overwhelming desire for us to be free of our consciousness of sin then 'peace' is His overwhelming desire to see us enter into His rest. The book of Hebrews is all about entering His rest; especially chapters three and four.[19]

But 'according to' implies an endless supply (which of course it is) and the provision is in measure to that limitless storehouse.

And Philippians chapter four is all about the *God of Peace* bringing the *Peace of God* into our lives. Peace as Paul understood it in the Hebrew language (Shalom) means completeness, soundness, welfare, prosperity, nothing missing, nothing broken, tranquility, contentment and rest. In other words, love and grace in action. The 95th Psalm (8-11) as well as the book of Hebrews equate the taking of the Promised Land to entering the rest (or peace) that God has provided for His family. *"Today, if you will hear His voice...let us therefore fear, lest a promise being left us of entering into His rest...should come short of it...for we which have believed do enter into rest"* Believing (faith) is the key. And that 'Promised Land' is not heaven. All of Hebrews chapter three speaks of the joys of entering that rest and then in chapter four He tells us to labor to enter into that rest. He's not telling us to work and look forward to dying. The last verse of chapter four tells us to come boldly before His throne to 'receive'. The message is *now*. His rest is *'today* if you will hear His voice'...Enter His rest.

And then the Holy Spirit by the Apostle tells us that we are blessed with all spiritual blessings. *"Certainly he is using a figure of speech. He can't mean 'all'* But if you research

_____
[19] Hebrews 3:8-12; 4:1-12

that word 'all' you will find that it means 'all'. And 'spiritual' does not mean something less that what we can see in this natural world. Remember, it was the Spiritual that created the 'natural'. And the things we see are temporal but the things we can't see are eternal.[20] But our flesh cries, *"Stop! This is too much"*[21]. But did you know that the God of Creation is the God of Too Much?

Those were Moses' exact words when the people needed to be restrained from giving for there was too *much.*[22]

And the woman whose sons were going to be sold for her dead husband's debts had the same experience when Elijah told her to borrow as many vessels as she could and pour from the small cruse of oil until they were all filled. She not only paid her debts but lived on the excess for the rest of her life.[23] And Jesus twice fed thousands with a parishioner's meager lunch. And the leftovers were enough to feed many more.[24] And a verse I'm sure you're familiar with goes like this, *"…and my God shall supply all your need according to His riches in glory"*[25] i.e., beyond your need.

He did not say *"…out of* His riches…" He said *'according to* His riches'. If it were 'out of His riches' then the supply is diminished. But *'according* to His riches' implies an endless supply (which of course it is) and the provision is in measure to that limitless storehouse. Startling? I hope so. And certainly allegorical to the religious (carnal) mind. But if you can receive it then your spirit will receive it, plant it and cause it to grow and eventually bear fruit in your life. Just don't root it up and kill it with words of unbelief (religion, tradition).

---

[20] 2 Corinthians 4:18

[21] If that has never been your heart's cry then you are not accepting literally what these simple words literally mean. The difference between a religious mindset and simple faith is being occasionally startled when you read God's Word.

[22] Exodus 36; Luke 6:38; Philippians 4:19

[23] 1 Kings 17

[24] Matthew 14, 15

[25] Philippians 4

So before we go any further with this section, receive His abundance of Love, Grace, Peace and Blessing. And rid your consciousness of the past so you can freely enjoy the Love of God and fellowship with your Father.[26]

Then say this if you dare *"I am holy, blameless, loved and chosen by Him before the foundation of the world."*.It's true you know. Just read verse four again.

[5] having predestined us to adoption as sons by Jesus Christ to Himself, according to the good pleasure of His will, [6] to the praise of the glory of His grace, by which He made us accepted in the Beloved. [7] In Him we have redemption through His blood, the forgiveness of sins, according to the riches of His grace [8] which He made to abound toward us in all wisdom and prudence, [Ephesians 1:5-8 NKJV]

What is God's will? We will get into that more deeply in the next section. But for now His will simply is to adopt us (you) in order to bring Him pleasure.

I know. That's blasphemous and not very religious. Certainly we're the ones who should be talking about pleasure; the immeasurable pleasure of heaven; the joy and humbling pleasure of what Jesus has done. But that is just a side issue to Him. The Father's pleasure and joy and indeed that of Jesus is that we can spend eternity with them both. Look up 'joy' in your concordance and see how many times Jesus speaks of His joy and the Father's joy (and ours) being made full

> ## Make no mistake. God's love for you is unsearchable.

Of course He said the same thing about our joy. And surely our joy is beyond expression. But imagine yourself in the familiar story that Jesus told not as the prodigal son but

---

[26] 1 Timothy 6:17; John 10:10; 1 Corinthians 2:9; Ephesians 3:20; Matthew 7:11, etc.

22

as his father (Luke chapter fifteen). The son is humbled, humiliated and willing to work as a hired hand on his father's farm. But the father… would not even hear his son's prepared confession. He ran and hugged his smelly neck and put a robe on his filthy, pig slop stained shoulders. Make no mistake. God's love for you is unsearchable.

God has pulled out all stops and made us not only acceptable but accepted. And not only 'accepted' but accepted in the Beloved.

Have you ever heard the last stanza of the old hymn, *"The Love of God"*? The author is not even known. But I could play it at high volume non-stop; each time moving an inch or so closer to its truth.

Could we with ink the oceans fill.
And were the skies of parchment made.
Were every stalk on earth a quill.
And every man a scribe by trade.
To write the love of God above
Would drain the oceans dry;
Nor could the scroll contain the whole,
Though stretched from sky to sky

Get the point? I won't even touch on John chapter seventeen where Jesus talks of that capacity for love being *in us.* We have too much to comprehend right here in Ephesians.

"To the praise of the glory of His grace." Maybe the Amplified Version can help us here:

So that we might be to the praise and commendation of His glorious grace, favor and mercy which He so freely bestowed on us in the Beloved. (AMP)

Ok, that's still pushing the envelope. But it's still all about Him. God has pulled out all stops and made us not only *acceptable* but *accepted*. And not only '*accepted*' but *accepted in the Beloved*.

> **Have you ever heard anyone say, "God's will is a mystery"?**

Do you get it? We are accepted in Him. In Whom? In the One whom God loves from eternity. We are of course accepted in Jesus. But there is more.

The Father already had Jesus. And though He loved Him He endured the cross '*...for the joy set before Him.'* The Father sent Jesus to be (permanently) like us so that He could spend eternity...with us...with you...and me.

The next verse expands on that concept *"...in whom we have redemption... forgiveness...and the riches of His grace."* And He has *"...abounded toward us in all wisdom and prudence."*

Wisdom is a vast enough subject by itself but 'prudence' adds "understanding and insight" (AMP)

Here we are with that little word 'all' again. How can we possibly have 'all' wisdom? And don't forget about 'redemption' and 'forgiveness' and the 'riches of His grace'. Well hang on because even greater stuff is coming.

But let's look at this.

It is not by natural thinking that these last few verses can be comprehended. 'Faith' is a much maligned concept in our society and even in our churches. Some call it 'mind over matter'. Others just sneer and call it 'positive thinking'. And some just avoid it altogether. But it simply means taking God at His Word. So find out what He said...and believe it. And the Author of our faith tells us that it is impossible to please God without it. See Hebrews 11:6.

You can read more about faith in the appendix at the end of the book. But for now just receive what God's Word says. That is God's definition of faith. Find out what He said, believe it, say it (confess it) and act on it. That's faith. You used it to get saved...and it's still there. Unbelief is natural.[27] Belief takes practice. So practice believing. And let the Love of God startle you.

Now we get into the really good stuff.

> *This was no well-placed sermon lead-in. He knew what was coming and this faith confession was as much to Himself as to His staff.*

[9] having made known to us the mystery of His will, according to His good pleasure which He purposed in Himself, [10] that in the dispensation of the fullness of the times He might gather together in one all things in Christ, both which are in heaven and which are on earth--in Him. [11] In Him also we have obtained an inheritance, being predestined according to the purpose of Him who works all things according to the counsel of His will, [12] that we who first trusted in Christ should be to the praise of His glory. [Ephesians 1:9-12 NKJV]

How would you like to know the mystery of God's will? Again, He has done that and more. He did it according to His own pleasure. He delights in you and I knowing not only His will but the 'mystery' of His will. Have you ever heard anyone

---

[27] This may seem unfair. But it's just like 'walking'. That comes pretty naturally. If you want to fly however you're going to have to study and practice things that don't come quite so naturally—but it's worth it.

say, "God's will is a mystery"? After all didn't Jesus say, "Not My will, but Thy will be done[28]"?

Did you also notice that Jesus knew exactly what the will of the Father was when He prayed that prayer? His was not a question of what God wanted. It was a heart rending statement of faith in what His Father had already revealed. What did He tell the disciples after cursing the fig tree? *"Have faith in God."*[29]

This was no well-placed sermon lead-in. He knew what was coming and this faith confession was as much to Himself as to His staff.

No, God's will is not a mystery. The 'mystery' (hidden *for* us, not *from* us) of His will has been gladly and joyfully made known to us because it gives Him pleasure to freely give us all things.

His plan all along has been to reconcile, unite, gather into one accord all, everyone in Christ, indeed all heaven and earth in Him.[30] In Whom we also have an inheritance. This is the love of God in action. The rest of this verse reiterates His plan, purpose, wisdom and will for us.[31] And the reason for His unspeakable gift: again, that we should be to His praise and enjoyment who have trusted in His Son.

[13] In Him you also [trusted], after you heard the word of truth, the gospel of your salvation; in whom also, having believed, you were sealed with the Holy Spirit of promise, [14] who is the guarantee of our inheritance until the redemption of the purchased possession, to the praise of His glory. [Ephesians 1:13-14 NKJV]

---

[28] Luke 22:42

[29] Mark 11:22

[30] This is a literal translation of verse ten which in itself is a mystery to translators and commentators. But using the intent of the context as well as its corresponding verses in Colossians 1:20 and 2 Corinthians 5:18-19; comparing scripture with scripture the passage becomes more clear.

[31] You will find that all of God's promises are repeated over and over in His Word (Covenant) for two reasons. First to make His will for us plain. And second to make sure we actually got the point. God's promises are typically beyond comprehension and therefore easily relegated to metaphor or set aside as something to be revealed in heaven after we die.

Faith comes by hearing. The Word of truth (or 'Word of faith' as Paul calls it by the Spirit in Romans 10:8) brought salvation and sealing of the Holy Spirit and earnest or promise, assurance of our inheritance and redemption in Christ. All of which leads to praise and glory in heaven and earth. Praise and glory are always the result of God's plan and purpose realized on His family.

> **If you are seeking change in your life then make verse 17 your daily devotion and confession.**

The Apostle's Spirit-inspired prayer is next. And it is the heart and soul of this power-packed revelation that some have called the pinnacle of the New Testament. So if you feel like things have been a little lofty so far, strap into your chair because it gets better.

[15] Therefore I also, after I heard of your faith in the Lord Jesus and your love for all the saints, [16] do not cease to give thanks for you, making mention of you in my prayers: [17] that the God of our Lord Jesus Christ, the Father of glory, may give to you the spirit of wisdom and revelation in the knowledge of Him, [Ephesians 1:15-17 NKJV]

Has anyone ever heard of your faith? I don't mean because you told them. I mean that they just 'heard of your faith.' I hope so. But without phones, electronic media or even regular postal service, Paul heard of the faith of those in the church at Ephesus. And here is his prayer for them in response: that they would receive the spirit of wisdom and revelation.

That is my prayer constantly. More than wisdom and more than revelation; Paul speaks of the 'spirit' of wisdom and revelation. If ever there were a spirit you and I should covet, this would be it. What if the spirit of wisdom were within you? Do you think that spirit would be in contact, even communion with God's Spirit? Would questions of His will and direction in your life be addressed with confidence? And would the spirit of revelation clear up any problem that tried to confound you?

You will need the spirit of wisdom and revelation just to get a glimpse.

If you are seeking change in your life then make verse 17 your daily devotion and confession. Spirits of all kinds are all about us; care, worry, depression, distraction, fear, unbelief, and bad news. That last one is not only audible but visible. Just pick up a newspaper or turn on the TV news. Limit those two and take a daily supplement (morning, noon and night is the recommended dosage) of the spirit of wisdom and revelation[32] and you will never be the same. I know you've heard that before. And I'll probably say it again. And you cannot possibly practice every wise aphorism you've ever heard. But this one you should. Say it. Receive it. Attach your name to it. Change will come.

[18] the eyes of your understanding being enlightened; that you may know what is the hope of His calling, what are the riches of the glory of His inheritance in the saints, [19] and what [is] the exceeding greatness of His power toward us who believe, according to the working of His mighty power [20] which He worked in Christ when He raised Him from

---

[32] How do you 'take' those doses? The same way you take a thought. According to Jesus when you give voice to your thoughts you 'take' them (Matthew 6:31). He was speaking of the negative but the same process works in the positive. 'Take' the spirit of wisdom and revelation by saying. Quote that verse throughout the day even. In fact any promise you have need of can be 'taken' the same way.

the dead and seated [Him] at His right hand in the heavenly [places], [Ephesians 1:18-20 NKJV]

The lifting of our consciousness into the heavenlies continues. Paul's prayer goes on into chapter two. But let's try to get our understanding around where his Spirit-led scripture-based prayer is leading us. You will need the spirit of wisdom and revelation just to get a glimpse.

In addition to verse seventeen we now are asked to believe (and receive) the eyes of our understanding being enlightened. And the reason? So we can know His hope and His calling (see Colossians 1:5 and Hebrews 3:1). And get a clear picture of our inheritance,.the riches and glory of it, that is. By the way do you know when you receive an inheritance? Some seem to think 'religiously' that it's in heaven when we die. But that's not true, is it? We receive our inheritance when the One who has willed the inheritance dies.[33]

Or do you just set it aside thinking, "I just can't handle (believe) this." Well, there is a solution.

Hebrews 9:14-17 makes this abundantly clear. Our inheritance is now. Jesus is the only testament (will) writer who is also the executor of His own will. Heaven will be glorious. But the inheritance of the blood-bought covenant promises established between Jesus and the Father is now. Jesus inherited everything. And we are heirs of God and

---

[33] This is a perfect example of what 'religious' thinking or 'tradition' can do to skew even the simplest of concepts (see Matthew 15:3-6; Mark 7:8-13; Colossians 2:8). Paul also uses 'tradition' in a positive sense but rather than contradicting Jesus' words, he is referring the the Spirit-led traditions given to the church by revelation.

joint-heirs with Jesus.[34] Stop waiting for heaven. You have God's love and blessing today.

And how about power. Paul is still praying that we receive understanding of the power that God released in us. "According to the working of His mighty power with which He raised Jesus from the dead!" I told you it got better.

> *Jesus is the only testament (will) writer who is also the executor of His own will.*

Our heads can't handle this. So do we allegorize what it says. Or do we just set it aside thinking, "I just can't handle (believe) this." Well, there is a solution.

Your spirit believes it. So let your spirit deal with it. Your spirit receives and believes what *you tell it*. If you give voice to the doubt and unbelief that your head is thinking then that is what your spirit believes. If on the other hand you give voice to the God-given words that the Apostle Paul has prayed then your spirit is committed to not only believe, but to act on what you say. But you and I can't say it just once and then spend the rest of the day voicing our inferiority, our fear and our insecurities (even in jest) and expect change.

Your head (flesh) may not feel like what you are saying (confessing) is true (or even possible) but this is not about feelings. This always makes more sense in the negative. Consider taking "worry" by saying it. Worry is simply faith in the negative outcome as opposed to the positive (calling those things that be not as though they were). Can worry or care, though not physical, cause a physical response? Change of hair color (appearance), disrupted digestive function (sickness), distraction from your current task (lack of peace)? If we believe that meditation in the negative brings physical manifestation, why would we not agree with our Creator that meditation on His promises can do the same (only positive)?

---

[34] Romans 8:17

Your spirit loves, believes and will work with God's Word and God's Spirit to bring to pass whatever you say that is in line with His will (i.e., what He has already said). Some refer (not necessarily kindly) to this as 'positive confession'.[35]

Well, the promises (inheritance) in God's Word are certainly positive. And certain 'positive' or 'happy' talk will actually have a good effect on your attitude and even your well being. But God's Word is not about 'happy'. It has the power within itself to bring to pass

> ## *Your spirit loves and believes, and will work with God's Word and God's Spirit to bring to pass whatever you say that is in line with what He has already said.*

God's purpose (will) in your life. Read Isaiah 55:10-11.

This digression from Ephesians chapter one is no accident. The final verses that follow as well as chapters 2-6 will take a well fed and matured spirit to even begin to get a handle on. Your spirit is fed by the Word of God. So the more you read, study, meditate and confess God's Word the stronger your spirit will become. So if you're ready let's look at the grand finale of chapter one.

[21] far above all principality and power and might and dominion, and every name that is named, not only in this age but also in that which is to come. [22] And He

---

[35] The difference between confessing the 'positive' and confessing God's Word about you is that one can produce change while the other produces what your Creator has already decreed about you. When the change is in the direction of who you were made to be then direction and the life of God comes with it.

put all [things] under His feet, and gave Him [to be] head over all [things] to the church, [23] which is His body, the fullness of Him who fills all in all.
[Ephesians 1:21-23 NKJV]

This is a continuation of the previous sentence. The picture is that of Jesus seated at the right hand of the Father and where that seat really is. "Far above…" You can read the rest. But pay attention to this: all things are under His feet…and He is the Head of the body. What body? Well, if you didn't know already He makes it more plain in chapter four as well as in more detail in First Corinthians chapter twelve. We are His body. We are the body of Christ.

> **But pay attention to this: all things are under His feet…and He is the Head of the body.**

So where then, are the principalities and powers, etc. and everything else that has a name?

They are under His feet. And His feet are in His body. So even if you're the big toe, they're all under you. Here is a perfect opportunity to exercise the literal understanding of scripture. The language here is obviously figurative.[36] So our job is to determine the literal truth intended by the figurative language[37]. We are in Christ and therefore walk in the authority and power rightly given Him.

He gave us that authority by giving us the use of His Name.[38] When you go on vacation and give power of

---

[36] I use the term 'figurative' here to help with our 'natural' understanding. In a 'supernatural (spiritual) sense this statement is literally true.

[37] But we are not free to assign any literal truth we imagine. Comparing scripture with scripture it becomes clear that the universal church or the collective body of born again believers around the world is the body of Christ. We are 'in Him' and therefore what He is, we are and what He possesses, we possess.

[38] More than a salutation or closing line of a prayer, God's view of His Name is that of His very nature. In the context of covenants the exchange of names is tantamount to mingling blood. *What is mine is now yours and your life, future, well being and family are now my responsibility.* David had that kind of covenant with Jonathan. And Mephibosheth (only indirectly connected to their bond)

attorney to your associate to conduct your business, you don't expect him to call every time a bill comes due or a problem needs to be settled. You gave him authority to use your name and take care of what you have already instructed (willed) him to do.

This does not mean that God is disconnected from our lives. It simply means that we are authorized to use the same Kingdom Process that Jesus used. While on earth He could do nothing of Himself.[39] He simply said what He heard His Father say.[40] And He did whatever He saw the Father do.

> *Then He left and sent the Holy Spirit to reside within us along with His authority (power of attorney) to accomplish the same process.*

Then He left and sent the Holy Spirit to reside within us along with His authority (power of attorney) to accomplish the same process in you and me![41] Four of the most powerful chapters in all of scripture (John 14-17) explain this process in detail.[42]

But this is about Ephesians so get ready for chapter two.

---

reaped the rewards as a member of Jonathan's family (see 2 Samuel chapter 9). The early disciples went beyond trusting Jesus and using the authority of His Name to having FAITH IN THE NAME itself (see Acts 3:16).

[39] John 5:19, 30

[40] John 14:10-31

[41] John 14:16-17; 16:13

[42] Make a habit of reading these four chapters regularly. In my Bible that's 5 pages. These are Jesus' final words on earth to His staff...and according to 17:20, to us. Also there is plenty here on which to use the spirit of wisdom and revelation that you received in Chapter one.

CHAPTER TWO
GOD'S BRAGGING RIGHTS

[1] And you [He made alive], who were dead in trespasses and sins, [2] in which you once walked according to the course of this world, according to the prince of the power of the air, the spirit who now works in the sons of disobedience, [3] among whom also we all once conducted ourselves in the lusts of our flesh, fulfilling the desires of the flesh and of the mind, and were by nature children of wrath, just as the others. [4] But God, who is rich in mercy, because of His great love with which He loved us, [5] even when we were dead in trespasses, made us alive together with Christ (by grace you have been saved), [6] and raised [us] up together, and made [us] sit together in the heavenly [places] in Christ Jesus, [7] that in the ages to come He might show the exceeding riches of His grace in [His] kindness toward us in Christ Jesus. [Ephesians 2:1-7 NKJV]

The first and last verses of this passage sum up Paul's message for the entire letter. You and I are made alive who once were dead in sins so that God could show off (and show us off) as to what He can accomplish through grace and kindness and through His love and His Son. That's why this chapter is about 'God's Bragging Rights'.

...so that God could show off (and show us off) as to what He can accomplish through Grace and kindness and through the love of His Son.

Our past was filled with conversation and companionship influenced by the enemy of our souls. That's harsh talk for most of us who smoked and joked and golfed and talked over sports news. And poked fun at ourselves, our finances, our wives (husbands) and our children and our country…and church folks. But surely not the demonic children of wrath that Paul is describing. His words *are* harsh. But the truth is that we are not sovereign. Only God is sovereign. God created man like Himself but dependent on Him.. When Adam sinned he gave up his dependence on God and submitted himself to his new god, satan. As Jesus put it, *"He that believeth on him is not condemned: but he that believeth not is condemned already…"* We serve one master or the other. If we are not purposely involved in God's Kingdom and His will for us and our world we default to the prince and power of the air and his kingdom of lies and deception. Does that mean we're lost? Well, Paul is certainly describing our lost condition prior to being 'quickened'. But as a quickened re-born spirit there is still a danger of wasting all of what God has made available through the sacrifice of His Son and the gift of His Spirit. Consider the Spirit's definition of faith, *"…he that comes to God must believe that He is and that He is a rewarder of them that diligently seek Him."*

> *Way beyond what we could ever ask or think or even imagine ...so don't try. This is "spirit" (heart) stuff not "mind" (head) stuff.*

It's that *"diligently seek Him"* part that always gets me. And once you grasp that, there is the part about being a *'rewarder'*.

If you and I are not diligently seeking Him then we'll probably scrape by, but the rest of the world will not.[43] Look

---

[43] There is more to our salvation than shunning hell and gaining heaven. When we allow apathy or religion to rob us of our privileges then we rob others of what

at Paul's next statement, *"But God, who is rich in mercy, for his great love wherewith he loved us…"*

Here we are back to the love of God again. If we really even begin to comprehend this concept…our conversation (and Word level) will change.

We were dead in sins yet He raised us up to sit together with Him in the very Throne Room of the Most High God. Way beyond what we could ever ask or think or even imagine…so don't try. This is 'spirit' stuff not 'mind' stuff. And why does He even bother?

> ## *Let us therefore come <u>boldly</u> to the Throne of Grace.*

Go back a couple of paragraphs. He's just showing off. And showing us off to the host of heaven. The angels have wondered at this God-offspring creation marvel since they first witnessed God duplicating Himself as recorded in Genesis 2:7.[44]

[8] For by grace you have been saved through faith, and that not of yourselves; [it is] the gift of God, [9] not of works, lest anyone should boast. [10] For we are His workmanship, created in Christ Jesus for good works, which God prepared beforehand that we should walk in them.
[Ephesians 2:8-10 NKJV]

This lofty passage is child's play compared to where we've come from. But think about that for a moment. If the saving grace of Almighty God at the expense of His perfect, spotless, sinless beloved Son is easily dealt with compared

---

God has called us to accomplish in their behalf.
[44] "In His image" = *"looks like Him"*.

And "in His likeness" = *"with His nature"*.

See Genesis 5:3 for an identical description of Seth compared to Adam. God did in fact duplicate Himself in Adam and Eve limited only by their dependence on God and lacking His sovereignty.

to where we've been...then we've been before the very Throne of God.

And that's exactly where God wants to take us. And it is His Word that will take us there...whenever we want. We're always welcome. Read Hebrews chapter four for yourself, but I'll just quote the last verse here, *"Let us therefore come boldly unto the Throne of Grace, that we may obtain mercy, and find grace to help in time of need."*

> *At that time you were without Christ ...and strangers from the Covenants of Promise having no hope and without God in the world.*

If you still feel that there is something we must do ("If I want to see the mayor of my less than 5k population town, I still need at least an appointment") then consider those 'good works' (verse 10); they are first and foremost whatever He says to do. But the highest of all good works is to obey the quote in the previous paragraph. To come 'boldly' can only mean that you know you are His favorite child[45] and that you have forsaken your old sin consciousness; being as comfortable in His presence as He is overjoyed to be in yours.[46]

[11] Therefore remember that you, once Gentiles in the flesh--who are called Uncircumcision by what is

---

[45] We all are. Another word for Grace is Favor.

[46] Does that offend your religious concept of God? Well, the purpose of this study is to begin to scratch the surface of our understanding of the love of God. Go back to the beginning and this time pray for the spirit of wisdom and revelation to shut down the limits of your imagination and open your spirit to all that His Spirit has to say.

called the Circumcision made in the flesh by hands--
[12] that at that time you were without Christ, being
aliens from the common-wealth of Israel and strangers
from the covenants of promise, having no hope and
without God in the world.
[Ephesians 2:11-12 NKJV]

The Apostle is speaking
to Jewish Christians (and by
extension to all of us) but the
message is clear. We were not
only without Christ but aliens to
the Commonwealth of Israel
(remember he's talking to
Jews…this is a strong
indictment). But the biggest
challenge (and also the strongest hope) follows: strangers
from the covenants of promise, hopeless and estranged from
God.

Bring heaven to an uproar of praise and the Father His greatest joy.

All of this is important because it is past tense (which
Paul expands on in the next few verses).

If you are a born again joint-heir with Jesus and a
favored (favorite) child of the Most High God then you are
with Christ. And if 'with Christ' then well known and accepted
into the commonwealth of Israel (the very seed of
Abraham).[47] and a blood sworn partner to the covenants of
promise. And if a blood sworn partner to the covenants of
promise then possessing an eternal, earnest expectation
and hope; and with God in the world.

If not, then receive the unfathomable love described
in these pages and bring heaven to an uproar of praise and
the Father His greatest joy. A prayer expressing this simple
but earth and heaven shaking decision can be found at the
beginning of this study.

[13] But now in Christ Jesus you who once were
far off have been brought near by the blood of Christ.

---

[47] Galatians 3:29

[14] For He Himself is our peace, who has made both one, and has broken down the middle wall of separation,

> ## *Now you are no more strangers and foreigners but fellow-citizens with the saints, and of the Household of God.*

[15] having abolished in His flesh the enmity, [that is], the law of commandments [contained] in ordinances, so as to create in Himself one new man [from] the two, [thus] making peace, [16] and that He might reconcile them both to God in one body through the cross, thereby putting to death the enmity. [17] And He came and preached peace to you who were afar off and to those who were near. [Ephesians 2:13-17 NKJV]

Made near by the blood of the Everlasting Covenant.[48] He is our Peace and he has abolished the enmity between heaven and earth. Do you remember the angel's pronouncement at Jesus' birth? *"Glory to God in the highest, and on earth peace, good will toward men".*

It was God's statement of faith that His will be done on earth as it is in heaven. Jews and non-Jews alike (that's everyone) are reconciled to God by the cross. Read the prophecy to which the Apostle is referring in Isaiah 52:7.

[18] For through Him we both have access by one Spirit to the Father. [19] Now, therefore, you are no longer strangers and foreigners, but fellow citizens with the saints and members of the household of God, [Ephesians 2:18-19 NKJV]

---

[48] Hebrews 13:20-21

Here is the Apostle's clear statement of where we are as opposed to where we were. Don't ever get the two mixed up.

Remember where we began this journey regarding the purging of even our consciousness (remembrance) of sin. We now have access to the Father (heaven, the Kingdom, the very Throne of God). No more strangers but *citizens* with all the rights of natural born subjects, heirs even, with the saints and more even than citizens...members of the household (family, residence) of God.

> *The Spirit of wisdom and revelation has its most profound effect on verses or passages we think we already know.*

God's promises (covenants) as you can see are repeated over and over. Especially the best and highest which we are certainly delving into in these passages. Don't take any of this lightly. Especially if these verses are familiar.

Read them again as if you have never read any of this before. The spirit of wisdom and revelation has its most profound effect on verses or passages we think we already know. But our part is to spend time here. Meditate on God's unthinkable blood-sworn oath to you. Whether your head likes the idea (or can even handle it) or not, your spirit knows it's true

But it just may take some time to get past the traditional and religious sentries long established in our un-renewed minds. We'll talk about this some more in chapter six but for the time being take your stand according to Second Corinthians 10:3-5.

For though we walk in the flesh, we do not war after the flesh: (For the weapons of our warfare are not carnal, but mighty through God to the pulling down of strong holds;) Casting down imaginations, and every high thing that exalts itself against the knowledge of God, and bringing into captivity every thought to the obedience of Christ;

> **The mind is the connection between the flesh and the spirit.**

Your spirit has been re-created (re-born) but your mind still needs to be renewed. And the reason that your mind can give you so much trouble… and the reason that the enemy's attacks are directed at the mind… is that the mind is the connection

> **It just may take some time to get past the traditional and religious sentries long established in our un-renewed minds.**

between the flesh and the spirit. More on this again in chapter six but know that the verse just quoted above is the surest way to accomplish what God's Word says on the subject in Romans 12:1-2.[49]

---

[49] Taking your thoughts captive according to 2nd Corinthians 10:3-5 is the process of renewing your mind in Romans 12:2. But you don't take thoughts captive by thoughts. Knowing your authority and speaking that authority is primary to renewing your mind. Death and Life are in the power of the tongue.

Now let's finish up chapter two and prepare to move from Mt. Everest into the heavenlies in chapter three.

20] having been built on the foundation of the apostles and prophets, Jesus Christ Himself being the chief corner[stone], [21] in whom the whole building, being fitted together, grows into a holy temple in the Lord, [22] in whom you also are being built together for a dwelling place of God in the Spirit.
[Ephesians 2:20-22 NKJV]

These last three verses sum up the 'purpose of the church' that Paul expands on in chapter four. So just know that the power given to the church on earth (you and me) has two conditions: 1) be rock-solidly founded on Jesus Christ as the Chief Cornerstone, and 2) that it be in unity.

We are probably pretty conscientious about number 1 but boy do we need work on number 2. And you can start working on it now before we even get to chapter four. 'Take' these three verses by confessing their truth (that by all appearances may not seem true) as if it were true and manifested in the earth. See Romans 4:17.

CHAPTER THREE
GOD'S LOVE WITHOUT LIMITS

[1] For this reason I, Paul, the prisoner of Christ Jesus for you Gentiles-- [2] if indeed you have heard of the dispensation of the grace of God which was given to me for you, [3] how that by revelation He made known to me the mystery (as I have briefly written already, [4] by which, when you read, you may understand my knowledge in the mystery of Christ), [5] which in other ages was not made known to the sons of men, as it has now been revealed by the Spirit to His holy apostles and prophets: [6] that the Gentiles should be fellow heirs, of the same body, and partakers of His promise in Christ through the gospel, [7] of which I became a minister according to the gift of the grace of God given to me by the effective working of His power. [8] To me, who am less than the least of all the saints, this grace was given, that I should preach among the Gentiles the unsearchable riches of Christ, [9] and to make all see what [is] the fellowship of the mystery, which from the beginning of the ages has been hidden in God who created all things through Jesus Christ; [Ephesians 3:1-9 NKJV]

> *In Whom we have boldness and access with confidence.*

In this rather lengthy introduction to chapter three—although you know Paul didn't write in chapters, right—he summarizes again his purpose in writing and repeats for our benefit the limitless promise of God to bless His family. All of which is a revelation about the unsearchable riches of Christ and the fellowship of (partnering in, partaking of) the mystery (His love for us) which was hidden and has now been revealed. He expands on this revelation starting with the next few verses.

[10] to the intent that now the manifold wisdom of God might be made known by the church to the principalities and powers in the heavenly [places], [11] according to the eternal purpose which He accomplished in Christ Jesus our Lord, [12] in whom we have boldness and access with confidence through faith in Him. [13] Therefore I ask that you do not lose heart at my tribulations for you, which is your glory.
[Eph. 3:10-13 NKJV]

> *The angels are made to serve and worship God. Just like us, right? Nope. Not even close. Service and worship are not God's highest priority.*

Listen to that tenth verse from the Amplified Version. *"The purpose is that through the church the complicated, many-sided wisdom of God in all its infinite variety and innumerable aspects might now be made known to the angelic rulers and authorities (principalities and powers) in the heavenly sphere."* (AMP)

Did you get that? The angels learn of the magnitude of the wisdom of God through the church. But the angels are made to serve and worship God. Just like us, right? *Not even close.* Service and worship are not God's highest priority. Angels are not family. They are created in a different class from God and not heir to His promises. Nor can they be.

A man may will his fortune to his cockatiel or goldfish. But he exhibits a skewed understanding of relationship, fellowship and certainly of kinship.

46

God, who understands these concepts better than anyone seeks to have offspring that He may love and bless. Therefore we, by His limitless grace, are made joint-heirs with His Son who has inherited all things. His wisdom is included in that inheritance and God's angel armies now look to the church (you and me) to know the revelation of His plan and purpose.

> *Angels are not family. They are created in a different class from God and not heir to His promises. Nor can they be.*

The most stunning revelation is of course that we have access with boldness and confidence that none of the rest of His creation enjoys. Angels are appointed to serve (minister) for those who shall be heirs of salvation.[50] And they are appointed to minister to God around His throne.[51] But they are not invited in of their own accord…and certainly not with boldness. Only His family is invited to sit[52] with Him in His throne. That is the wisdom and revelation that principalities and powers (angels) they seek to know through the church.

"Wherefore," Paul says, *"don't worry about me. I am partaker of all I have just revealed to you."*[53] To have access where angels fear to tread; and to look forward to an eternity enjoying that access is so overwhelming to him that all his tribulation is nothing compared to the unsearchable grace and love of God.

Paul's comfort and consolation for those given into his care continues. What was beyond comprehension in chapter

---

[50] Hebrews 1:14; Psalm 91:11
[51] Revelation 7:11-12; Isaiah 6:1-3
[52] Ephesians 2:6
[53] Ephesians 3:13

one and even higher in chapter two now enters the rare air of the stratosphere. I promise I won't say that again. This is as good as it gets (which is of course untrue because we will never reach that point). But brace yourself anyway.

[14] For this reason I bow my knees to the Father of our Lord Jesus Christ, [15] from whom the whole family in heaven and earth is named, [16] that He would grant you, according to the riches of His glory, to be strengthened with might through His Spirit in the inner man, [17] that Christ may dwell in your hearts through faith; that you, being rooted and grounded in love, [18] may be able to comprehend with all the saints what [is] the width and length and depth and height-- [19] to know the love of Christ which passes knowledge; that you may be filled with all the fullness of God. [Ephesians 3:14-19 NKJV]

We are named after the Father. Of course we are. We're family. But before we go any further with this you might want to meditate on that 'family' idea. We throw it around without thinking because we've heard it sung, quoted and mentioned in passing. But imagine yourself raiding your Father's fridge. Certainly your earthly family members might expect that. But God? You see, He is more serious about this 'family' thing than we've ever thought. If you have kids and love them then you begin to understand. But did you lose access and fellowship for thousands of years and then give up your only remaining Son who had been with you for eternity in a final attempt to reach out to what you lost. This truly, "win-or-lose-all" plan (mystery) leaves no way out. But you deem it worth everything to regain your beloved family.

> *If you're ok with that then you haven't got it yet.*

The gospels don't reveal all of this but First Corinthians 2:6-10 gives us a glimpse (and of course thank God for 'Ephesians' which attempts to reveal the rest).

In verse sixteen he seeks on our behalf, strength to receive what he is about to say. *"That Christ may dwell in your hearts by faith"* No surprise there. *"and that you being rooted and grounded in love"* Here it comes. *"may be able to comprehend [the four dimensional] love of Christ which passes knowledge that you may be filled…"* Are you ready? *"…with all the fullness of God."*

> ***Our religious solution is to ask timidly to protect our pride in case it doesn't work.***

If you're ok with that then you haven't got it yet. Let's go to the Amplified Version for verse nineteen to see if that startles you.

"That you may really come to know practically, through experience for yourselves, the love of Christ which far surpasses mere knowledge without experience; that <u>you may be filled through all your being unto all the fullness of God may have the richest measure of the Divine Presence, and become a body wholly filled and flooded with God Himself</u>." (AMP)

> ***"According to your faith be it unto you."***
> ***—Jesus***
> ***"Be it unto me according to Your Word."***
> ***—our response***

As one who has delved into this subject deeper than any I know, Brother Copeland would say, *"If that doesn't light your fire, your wood is wet!"*

Let's try to finish chapter three and get into the less lofty (but equally as powerful—and in need of the spirit of wisdom and revelation to receive) chapters four through six.

[20] Now to Him who is able to do exceedingly abundantly above all that we ask or think, according to the power that works in us, [21] to Him [be] glory in the church by Christ Jesus to all generations, forever and ever. Amen. [Ephesians 3:20-21 NKJV]

Now that we have stretched our minds and spirit to see (receive, believe) the extremities of God's love (passion) for us, the Apostle takes us one step further. Verse twenty tells us that His love goes beyond 'caring' to 'doing'. *He is able to 'do' exceeding abundantly beyond even our imaginations.* And then referring back to chapter one, he reminds us of the only limitation is the power that works within us (according to the power He used when He raised Jesus from the dead)...remember?[54]

Did you get that? You don't need spine-tingling, goose-flesh, hair-raising faith! You just need to know His Word is true...and say so.

Jesus told two blind beggars that their faith would determine their outcome.[55] And the Holy Spirit by Paul tells us that the outcome is *"...according to the power that works in us."*[56]

Two lines of scripture changed my view of faith recently when I got to know the main characters in this account.[57] Those lines are, 1. *"According to your faith be it unto you"* and 2. *"Be it unto me according to your word."*

---

[54] Ephesians 1:19-20
[55] Matthew 9:27-30
[56] Ephesians 3:20
[57] That's what meditation and revelation will do for you.

I don't like to be told that *I'm* the limitation. But that is the revelation I got when I looked in earnest at this passage. So let's look at those 'beggars' faith' and 'the power that works within us.'

The beggars' 'faith' amounted to six important steps: **1) Waiting** for Jesus (they were after all blind. They couldn't do much else. But they *did* do what they could. **2) Crying out** to Jesus. They were committed. **3) Following** Jesus. They didn't give up when their answer wasn't immediate. **4) Finding** Jesus. They sought Him out in the house (no small task for two blind guys in a crowd). **5) Asking**. Here is where some of us falter. Seems easy, but by asking we are putting our faith (and by some misunderstanding of relationship—*our reputation*) on the line. 'Asking' involves believing (faith). And our religious solution is to ask timidly and with reservation. *"If it be Thy will"* or some such unbelieving confession to protect our pride in case it doesn't work.[58] But then comes the clincher. **6) Answering**. Jesus said, *"Do you believe that I am able to do this?"* What possible difference does that make? Apparently a lot because Jesus asked. They answered, *"Yes, Lord."* And they were healed.

> *...so we can calmly and confidently say, "Be it unto me according to Your Word!"*

Did you notice that their answer again contained no unbelieving reservation such as *"I believe you can, but..."* or *"For someone else maybe but I'm too unworthy."* Then, and only then did Jesus pronounce, *"According to your faith be it unto you."*

---

[58] Yes, I know those were Jesus' words. But they were not spoken in unbelief or ignorance of God's will. He knew exactly what the Father's will was. And since it involved separating an eternal bond His mind wanted to rebel but His Spirit spoke those now infamous words, "Not My will but what You will." The Love of God accomplished the unthinkable...and we were made accepted in the Beloved.

Knowledge, action, determination and confession defined the faith that Jesus honored. But do you know what in one word got Jesus' attention? They *asked*. That is what takes faith. I know. I have struggled with that very concept. Whether taking the time to research the answer so that I can ask intelligently, or humbling myself to ask another to pray (agree) with me, asking takes faith. And you know what else...'asking' releases faith.

Let me repeat those two simple eight-word phrases that will move mountains in your life and bring you the desires of your heart.

"According to your faith be it unto you" and *"Be it unto me according to your word"*

The first was spoken by Jesus. The second by His mother before He was born. The results in both cases were undeniable and startling.

Here's how to apply this simple lesson to bring similar results to your situation. See Jesus saying to you, *"According to your faith be it unto you."* He is saying that, you know. And I know that you're thinking that pesky 'faith' qualifier rules you out. Well that's where the second statement comes in. *"Be it unto me according to Your Word."*

Did you get that? You don't need spine-tingling, goose-flesh, hair-raising faith. You just need to know His Word is true; *and say so*. He is the One who gave the promise and then sealed it in blood...so we can calmly (and confidently) say, *"Be it unto me according to Your Word."*

In other words, What you believe is God's Word. And you don't need to work up mountain moving faith. You are simply saying, *"I agree with you, Jesus. Be it unto me!"* That simple statement of faith from your heart will unleash the *"power that works within us."*

And the last verse speaks for itself, "*Unto Him be glory in the church by Christ Jesus throughout all ages, world without end. Amen."* And Amen!

Which leads us very nicely into *The Love of God* chapter four. For three chapters we have seen just a glimpse of what His love for us really means. Now we are about to experience how He intends for that love to affect our daily lives.

First, in the church; then in our families, then in the workplace (yes, your job) and then the grand finale. We will see just how complete and powerful His love is. No enemy can stand against it...and no weapon formed against it shall prosper.

CHAPTER FOUR
GOD'S PLAN FOR THE CHURCH

[1] I therefore, the prisoner of the Lord, beseech you that ye walk worthy of the vocation wherewith ye are called, [2] With all lowliness and meekness, with longsuffering, forbearing one another in love; [3] Endeavouring to keep the unity of the Spirit in the bond of peace. [4] [There is] one body, and one Spirit, even as ye are called in one hope of your calling; [5] One Lord, one faith, one baptism, [6] One God and Father of all, who [is] above all, and through all, and in you all.
[Ephesians 4:1-6 KJV]

> *Unto every one of us is given grace according to the measure of the gift of Christ.*

"*Therefore*" refers back to the previous three chapters. Now that we know (or have begun to know) how much we are loved by God...we can begin to live the love life. Which eliminates strife and results in unity which is the subject of the rest of this chapter. The seven '*ones*' in the next few verses emphasize the importance of unity in heaven and earth. It is a spiritual force that no enemy of God's plan, purpose, will, Word and people can stand against.

[7] But unto every one of us is given grace according to the measure of the gift of Christ. [8] Wherefore he saith, When he ascended up on high, he led captivity captive, and gave gifts unto men. [9] (Now that he ascended, what is it but that he also descended first into the lower parts of the earth? [10] He that descended is the same

also that ascended up far above all heavens, that he might fill all things.) [Ephesians 4:7-10 KJV]

We all have the gift of grace to the same measure as Christ. In other words at His resurrection He gave us that gift of grace…*His* grace.

> ## *Where he interferes now is as a thief and a liar and an outlaw and only with our consent.*

He went to hell and spoiled principalities and powers and rulers of the darkness and spiritual hosts of wickedness. He then returned to us all that He took back from the devil and the region of the damned. The gates of hell did not prevail against Him. He even made a show of them openly, triumphing over them in it. Now He fills all things that were once the domain and dominion of satan.[59]

From the first Adam's high treason until the resurrection[60] of the Last Adam (Jesus) satan and his forces occupied (held title deed to) planet earth. Where he interferes now is as a thief and a liar and an outlaw and only with our consent[61]

I emphasize this core truth of the gospel to set the stage for our instruction in how to walk in the victory Jesus won for us. Those instructions are covered in detail in the remaining chapters.

[11] And He Himself gave some [to be] apostles, some prophets, some evangelists, and some pastors

---

[59] Colossians 2:15; Ephesians 4:8

[60] Or more accurately, 50 days later at Pentecost. The battle was won at the resurrection clearing the way for God's Spirit and angel armies to re-populate the earth on the exact day commemorating the giving of the law under the Old Covenant. Pentecost now commemorates the giving of the Spirit under the New Covenant.

[61] The devil is a liar and the father of it. Deception is his only weapon. John 8:44; Revelation 12:9

and teachers, [12] for the equipping of the saints for the work of ministry, for the edifying of the body of Christ, [Ephesians 4:11-12 NKJV]

Having spoiled[62] principalities and powers, Jesus set up His elite troops and occupation forces with a five-fold leadership. *Their job*: the perfecting of the troops. *And their job?* the work of the ministry. *For what purpose?* the edifying (unifying) of the body of Christ.

The reason He gave apostles, prophets, evangelists, pastors and teachers was so that the saints could learn how to be perfected and do the work of the ministry. We'll talk some more in the following sections about how that works but these first two steps are critical.

1) *"...perfecting of the saints..."* And yes, He said 'perfecting'. Not just 'maturing' or 'getting better', *perfecting*. Modern Bible versions don't like that translation, but apparently Matthew, Paul, James, John and the writer of the book of Hebrews, did. The Greek language is very clear meaning 'perfecting' or 'fully equipped'.

> *Faith is believing God's promise (with your spirit [heart]) and grace is how He delivers on that promise to you (in this natural world).*

For us to comprehend this 'mystery' it will help to reflect that the Bible is a spiritual book. That does not make it irrelevant in the natural world. In fact the 'Spiritual' created the 'physical' so the spiritual world is more real than what we can experience all around us with

---

[62] ...to strip, despoil, disarm.. Colossians 2:15

our physical senses. The Spirit through the writer of the book of Hebrews explains it this way, *"...the worlds were framed by the word of God, so that things which are seen were not made of things which do appear."[63]* And through the Apostle Paul He said, *"...we look not at the things which are seen, but at the things which are not seen: for the things which are seen are temporal; but the things which are not seen are eternal."[64]*

> ## It is not the preparation that brings the warfare any more than it is the parenting classes that bring conflict.

So '*spiritual*' does not mean that it doesn't apply or that we can make up metaphors and similes to make it mean anything we want. We even have a religious term for that 'made up' kind of interpretation: '*spiritualize*'.

But 'spiritual' means simply that there is more in here about the spirit than about the flesh. God is a Spirit and so are you. You also have a soul (your mind, will and emotions) and you live in a body. It is your spirit that got born again and baptized into God's Holy Spirit. Which explains why with some the experience of salvation is accompanied with warm feelings and strong emotions and with others not at all.

Those feelings are not from your spirit. Your spirit just knows that it has been re-created and is now in perfect harmony and direct fellowship with God's Spirit. Your spirit-man is able to reside and commune with the Almighty because it is perfected, sin-free and made the very righteousness of God in Christ.

When God's Word speaks about 'you' the reference is usually to the spirit (which is the real you). When the reference is to the 'flesh' then the writer is speaking of your mind, your will and your emotions. References to the

---

[63] Hebrews 11:3
[64] 2 Corinthians 4:18

physical body are made clear whenever that is what is intended. *"Bodily exercise profits little"* is a typical example; or the description of the physical torture and abuse that Jesus endured leading up to and including a lingering and painful death on the cross.

But the spiritual torture goes inexplicably beyond even the horrors of the physical suffering. And the agony at Gethsemane foretells Jesus' separation from the Father as greater suffering than what He faced in His flesh. So your soul and flesh (physical body) are unique parts of your makeup and dependent on your spirit for their life.[65]

> *To be a 'doer' of the Word you simply first need to find out what it says ...and do it.*

And Paul's revelation of the body as the temple of the Holy Spirit shows that the flesh is the building in which our soul and spirit (and God's Spirit) reside. The writers mentioned above understood the difference. And Jesus almost always spoke of and addressed the spirit man.

So the 'perfecting' of the saints really does have reference to 'perfection' as it is generally understood. As we connect more and more to our spirit which has been re-created (made perfect) and able to stand continually in the presence of a Holy God our flesh is transformed by the renewing of our mind (soul). Your flesh may have a long road ahead to live out the life that is in your re-born spirit but as you will find in this study it is not a struggle. *It is of faith that it might be by grace* (Romans 4:16)[66].

Oh that we understood the depth of meaning in those two simple terms. *Faith* is believing God's promise (with your spirit) and *Grace* is how He delivers on that promise to you

---

[65] James 2:26; John 6:63; Proverbs 4:20-23 (heart=spirit)
[66] See also Matthew 11:28-30.

(in this natural world). How different our preaching and fellowship and study of God's marvelous Word would be with that revelation. This is the first task (purpose) of the five-fold ministry and our first responsibility (purpose) as members of the body of Christ—the glorious and victorious church.[67]

2) "...for the work of the ministry..."

If our religion gets us to church once or twice a month or even every week with no Word or faith exercise in between then we're no better off than the Pharisees.

The work of the ministry is to be orchestrated and taught by those called into that position. But they alone cannot accomplish all that needs to be done. The real work is to be done by the saints trained and perfected by the Spirit of the Living God and the five-fold ministry that He has given for that purpose.   You see, 'church' should be the coming together of the soldiers of the army of God to share our victories and our struggles and to comfort and encourage and to heal one another from the warfare of the previous week. We are after all, the 'victorious church' and wherever the victory is not evident in others then that brother or sister should be the focus of our encouragement—not our rejection and gossip.

A friend and brother in Christ many years ago had the odd habit to 'sniff' other believers when gathered for fellowship and before addressing the group. Anyone that was new would certainly ask, "What on earth is he doing?"

---

[67] Some would have us believe that the 'church' is the leadership and our part is to show up and so what they say...or what they say the Bible says. But Scripture knows nothing of this definition. To the Holy Spirit the 'church' is the body of Christ; the corporate bond of all true believers; and those for whom Christ will return on that day. It is us.

He would then often begin his message with the explanation that he was "smelling the smoke of battle" on those whom he knew to be engaged in the ongoing good fight of faith.

What some churches have become however is not at all what Jesus or the Holy Spirit intended—they have become a social gathering together to experience four songs, a few announcements, an offering and a twenty minute exposition of God's Word or entertaining homilies and metaphors.

> *You can edify the body of Christ by simply sharing with someone what you read earlier today.*

The only description we have recorded of a first century church service is about participation of the body of Christ.[68] Preaching though not mentioned there is obviously of primary importance and the Holy Spirit through Paul gave us simple instruction on what that is to be. *"Preach the word; be instant in season, out of season; reprove, rebuke, exhort with all longsuffering and doctrine"*.[69]

The most 'noble' of all believers were in a little town called Berea. They spent their week studying and searching the Word to confirm what they heard preached.[70]

Twenty five minutes a week (even if it *is* God's Word and not just clever stories) is not enough to get you through. One meal a week will not sustain your spirit. Especially if that week is comprised of your job, some TV and an occasional tirade about the weather, the government, your boss, your children (or your spouse), your neighbors and the preacher.

---

[68] 1 Corinthians 12-14
[69] 2 Timothy 4:2
[70] Acts 17:11

If you're not ready for open warfare then spend your week preparing.[71] Load up on the Word, not sitcoms. Find out what Jesus meant by doing, *"...greater works than these"* and what Paul meant by, *"I have fought a good fight."*[72] Then you will also find out what it means, *"...I am come that they might have life, and that they might have it more abundantly."*[73]

> **Jesus said that out of the abundance of the heart the mouth speaks; and what you say orders the circumstances around your life.**

Some let the discussion of 'warfare' in the Bible discourage them from living the full life that God has provided through Jesus. The truth is that the warfare is already here. If you are letting that keep you down then know two things. 1) Jesus paid a terrible price to put you over the enemy and his wiles (strategies) and 2) By not exercising our rights and privileges as an heir of God and joint heir with Jesus Christ as victor over all our circumstances we diminish what He accomplished.

I know that's harsh but it needs to be said. As passive or carnal believers in God's army we could very possibly fit the description of the 'lukewarm' churchgoer that Jesus spoke of in The Revelation.[74]

But don't despair. The doer of the Word that Jesus and James spoke of does not mean (necessarily) that you are to stand on the street corner with a bullhorn or scotch tape a gospel tract to the forehead of every sinner you pass. To be a 'doer' of the Word you simply first need to find out

---

[71] It is not the preparation that brings the warfare any more than it is the parenting classes that bring conflict. The warfare and the conflict are already present. But if we prepare then the battle (and the parenting) are not nearly as potentially devastating.

[72] What Paul means by a 'good fight' is one that is already won (Colossians 2:15)

[73] John 10:10

[74] Revelation 3:16

what the Word says…and do it; like walking in the privileges and authority that He won for us. But more on that later. Now let's look at what the work of the ministry really is. Here is what the Body of Christ is supposed to be doing.

3) *"…for the edifying of the body of Christ…*

" Hebrews 3:13 says, *"…exhort one another daily, while it is called To day; lest any of you be hardened through the deceitfulness of sin."*[75] You can't do that if you practice a Sunday-only faith. We are to edify the body of Christ. That means to encourage, exhort, strengthen and build up. This is a very important part of becoming a 'doer' of the Word. The rest of it is rather simple.

      Jesus made a pivotal statement about this process in Luke chapter six. He criticized the *religious* folks for painstakingly going about their *religious* duties. But then said that one who hears the Word and does not act on it is like a fool. His house, built on a sand foundation was destroyed beyond recognition when the storm came. And if you are old enough to feed yourself you know that the storms will come.

      So what is the difference? If our religion gets us to church once or twice a month or even every week with no Word or faith exercise in between then we're no better off than the Pharisees. But if you search the Word daily and believe in your heart what you find there and confess what it promises you with your mouth, you're on the road to building your house on the rock (see Romans 10 and Luke 6).

      You can edify the body of Christ by simply sharing with someone what you read earlier today. My brother is an expert at this. He will call with some gem he just encountered or some application of a familiar scripture that he just discovered. And I'm not the only one he tells. He'll strike up a conversation with a stranger at the restaurant or

---

[75] 'Deceitfulness of sin' does not necessarily refer to a life of crime or degradation. Our 'sin consciousness' is a more prevalent problem. Go back to the beginning for a refresher (and solution) regarding this problem.

the checker at the grocery store or share with someone at work or one of his clients. The point is that once it gets in you in abundance, the Word creates its own motivation (and opportunity).

And even if your efforts don't seem all that life changing, know two things. 1) God's Word never returns void; so your efforts are not empty (vain). You just may not see the immediate results, and 2) you are the joint beneficiary of sharing the Word. Your hearer is blessed because that Word is alive and caused to bear fruit according to the level described in Mark chapter four. That Word then becomes rooted in your heart and spirit and gives you a powerful (edifying) testimony *and* you have just become a doer of the Word.

> *How does that thirty three year span in light of all of history change the way I think or believe or live?*

[13] Till we all come in the unity of the faith, and of the knowledge of the Son of God, unto a perfect man, unto the measure of the stature of the fulness of Christ: [Ephesians 4:13 KJV]

4) *"...till we all come in the unity of the faith...*

" Have you noticed that 'unity' is not predominately the case within the church, or the body of Christ? How can they know we are Christians by our love (unity) when what they notice above all is our squabbles (strife)? Well, you can change all that. Yes, you. Well, you and me. You see, God has always had His man or woman.

God didn't slay Goliath. Well, actually of course He did. But He didn't do it without his man, David. And God didn't deliver the Jewish people from annihilation without His woman, Esther. And then there is Moses; and Ruth; and

Paul; and Stephen. *"But I'm not like any of those people!"* Actually if you're a born again, Spirit baptized believer you're right. You're *not* like them. You're better. Better (off, if you will) than the Old Testament saints because of your 'Better Covenant'. And better (off) than Paul and Stephen because we have their experience and testimony to encourage us.

> **They are exactly the same being, structure, species and physical makeup. They even look like you. Adam was no different.**

Jesus said that no prophet was greater than John the Baptist. But the least in the Kingdom is greater than he. I don't know it you're the least in the Kingdom (I doubt it) but even if you were you're still greater than the one of whom Herod said[76] when he heard of Jesus' miracles, *"...that John the Baptist was risen from the dead, and therefore mighty works do shew forth themselves in him."*

Jesus went on to say in John 14:12 that the works that He does you will do also and greater works will you do because He goes to the Father. So here is a mighty work that you can do—Love. Make a firm, quality, no turning back decision to walk in love. Study up on the subject. Find out what the Word has to say. Then do it. And if you slip (and you may)[77] then confess according to 1 John 1:9, receive your forgiveness and your cleansing and move on.

---

[76] Mark 6:14

[77] I did not say, "probably will". While that certainly is at least historically true, it needn't be of you and me. The lesson here (at least to me) is to watch my tongue and only say things that I expect the High Priest of my confession to actually oversee and bring to pass.

The lesson of First Corinthians chapter thirteen may seem like a daunting goal. But just try this. The love of God is in you according to John chapter 17 and 1 John chapters 1-5 so now you can read 1 Corinthians 13:4-8 and substitute your name wherever you see 'love' (or 'charity'). Stop after the first thought in verse eight ("…love never fails."). That sixty word confession repeated three times will take you about one minute. If you do that before you go to work or start your day for one week you will be amazed at the results. Maybe not in changing the world but certainly in changing you. I know. It changed (and is still changing) me.

> *This is such a radical concept that God calls those transformed by its power a new creation.*

Both Paul and Jesus were very strong on the spoken Word. The Father said by Jesus that "…out of the abundance of the heart the mouth speaks;" And what you say orders the circumstances around your life.[78] And the Spirit said by the Apostle Paul that "...with the heart one believes unto righteousness, and with the mouth confession is made unto salvation.".[79] And God's Spirit in Hebrews tells us that Jesus is the High Priest of our profession (confession)[80]. And Jeremiah quotes the Most High God saying, *"...I will watch over My Word to perform it."*[81] God is Love. And we have been given the ability to walk in that love. So meditate on and confess His Word. Then spread the Word.

This is what the 'unity of the faith' is all about.

5) *"...the knowledge of the Son of God...*

---

[78] Matthew 12:34-35 NKJV author's paraphrase
[79] Romans 10:10 NKJV
[80] Hebrews 3:1 KJV
[81] Jeremiah 1:12 KJV

Do you know more about Jesus today than when you were in Sunday School? When I was saved many years ago I think I knew *less* than I knew in Sunday School. During those years growing up (so to speak) I never knew that Jesus or God or the Bible or church or 'religion' had anything to do with my real life. Religion or church was for Sunday and real life was 24/7.

What a shock when I discovered that this Jesus that I had 'outgrown' years before was not only real He was very much interested in what I called my 'real life'. He was interested in my relationships, my fears, my weaknesses, my passion, my temper, my future and even my finances, my business, my family and my health. He was even interested in spending time with me…if I would just take the time to spend time with Him.

> *He's not improving the old. He is re-creating a whole new race.*

Did you know that when you separate yourself for a moment (on purpose) just to let Him know you appreciate Him, or even to say thanks for a beautiful day, or for a good deal at work...He doesn't frown and say, "It's about time." No. He turns to Jesus or one of the angels and with a bright smile says, "That's my girl [boy]!"

You don't need a life changing victory to get His attention. He's just excited to hear from you. Does that sound presumptuous or demeaning to refer to God in that way?

Well, if it does, then that's a sign you need to get rid of that sin consciousness we've been talking about. He loves you so much that if the 'world' that He sent His Son to save consisted of just you He wouldn't have changed a thing. *"Take My yoke upon you and learn of Me."* He said, *"for I am meek and lowly and you shall find rest for your soul."*

"Learn of Me..." The <u>knowledge of the Son of God</u>. Let's see, we know He was born in Bethlehem. We know He preached and taught for three years and then was executed. And then apparently rose from the dead. But what does that exactly mean to me? How does that thirty-three year span in light of all of history change the way I think or believe or live (other than that I know...or at least I'm pretty sure that I'm going to heaven...whatever that means). You may not be wholly connected to that last statement but the vast majority of the organized church today are. And if you and I are honest we'll find ourselves in there somewhere. Well, let me summarize what that thirty-three years means to us and what we need to know about the Son of God.

> *But let patience have her perfect work, that you may be perfect and entire, wanting nothing(!)*

Paul calls Jesus the 'last Adam' so let's start with the first Adam—created in the image and likeness of God. Theologians have tried for centuries to make this 'metaphor' understandable. Well, according to scripture it's no metaphor. God created an 'offspring'. He created a being like Himself. Much like your offspring are like you. Your children are no metaphor of who you are. They are exactly the same being, structure, species and physical makeup. They even look like you. Adam was no different. Everything God possessed Adam possessed.[82] See Genesis 5:7 again to see if a metaphor was intended.

The God of Creation became a 'Father' to His firstborn creation. Remember that phrase. We'll come back to it. Before long though, a 'thief' came in and stole Adam's allegiance. And the 'father of lies' became the illegitimate father of God's beloved offspring (see John 8:44). By

---

[82] ...except God's sovereignty. Man was made dependent...in need of a spiritual head. This begins to explain some of the devastation that took place starting in Genesis chapter three, and Jesus' startling declaration in John 8:44.

corrupting Adam, the enemy corrupted all of Adam's seed. Everyone born after Adam then was separated from his true Father by Adam's treason. Satan, by usurping Adam's position and authority gained title deed to everything Adam owned—and he owned it all. God didn't hold anything back. Remember that, too. We'll definitely come back to that.

Without even direct access to His cherished creation, God found Himself on the outside looking in. After Adam everyone knew that 'heaven' was separated from 'earth'[83]. Since Adam relinquished the dominion and authority by giving up all he had been given to voluntarily serve a ruthless, lying foreign master, God would have to find a man who would voluntarily (by faith) serve Him. And by him bring into the earth a man of God's own blood and species who would be able to pay for Adam's high treason.[84] But the catch was that he would in the process take back the dominion and authority and ownership that Adam lost.

That man was Abraham and the second man or Last Adam was of course Jesus. First Corinthians 2:6-9 explains this 'catch'. Verse eight is the key. All satan wanted was to get this trouble-making 'Messiah' out of the way. He thought the best way was to kill him. Well, by killing Jesus, the spotless, sinless, perfect offspring (sacrificial lamb) of God was ushered into the regions of the damned. It is there that He by faith conquered the devil and his minions and led captivity captive.[85]

That group he led out of there included Abraham, David, Moses and anyone else whose heart was inclined toward righteousness, who trusted in the God of Creation and looked forward to His Messiah. So Jesus did more than just die for our sins, as if that weren't enough. He

---

[83] Now you see why Jesus' statement in His 'model' prayer, "Thy kingdom come. Thy will be done as in heaven so in earth" Luke 11:2

[84] With an earth-body born of a woman (legally entitled to represent the first Adam) and with the blood of God; untouched by Adam's sin-tainted seed, this virgin-born miracle finally met all the requirements to reclaim man's lost kingdom and God's lost family.

[85] "Re-captured His own and led them to freedom"

took back everything Adam lost in the fall; dominion, fellowship, ownership, sonship, peace and access to God, heaven and His throne room. He's not holding anything back. I told you we'd come back to that. What Jesus restored was nothing less than the blessing originally bestowed on Adam. This is such a radical concept that God calls those transformed by its power a new creation. And He calls Himself their Father.

A new race of being. A new adoption or restoration into God's family. He calls this work that Jesus does in you being made the very righteousness of God. Or in Jesus' words, *"...new wine can't be put back into old bottles (skins)."* He's not improving the old, He is re-creating a whole new race. This restoration into God's original family that took four millennia to unfold can be called nothing less than being re-born, born again or born from above (God's Kingdom).

After the gospels Jesus is no longer called 'the only begotten Son of God'. He is called the First Born from the dead or the First Born of many brethren.[86] Jesus' spirit died (was separated from the Father) on that cross (see Psalm 22:1). And when He was raised from the dead He was begotten of the Father[87] (see Acts 13:33). Jesus was born again to new life when He was raised from the dead and He lives today to bring many sons (offspring) to glory (Hebrews 2:10). I told you we'd come back to that, too.

The idea of Jesus being a man and even more radically, a born-again man is not only new but blasphemous to some. But don't take my word for it. The Holy Spirit through the psalmist declares *"...Thou art my Son; this day have I begotten thee."* And that same Spirit by the Apostle Paul makes it clear by quoting that very passage (Psalm 2:7) that He is speaking of His resurrection (re-birth) from the depths of hell and not His being born of Mary in Bethlehem (Acts 13:33). If that is not enough then the Spirit through the writer of the book of Hebrews refers to Jesus' resurrection as being brought into the world 'again' after being given a name above all names.

---

[86] Romans 8:29; Colossians 1:15, 18; Hebrews 12:23
[87] "Again" according to Hebrews 1:5-6

And then, as already mentioned, there is the inescapable fact that Jesus is no longer called the *Only Begotten Son of God* but the *First Born from the dead* and the *First Born of many brethren.* If that doesn't startle you then you are not considering the ramifications of a born-again Man seated at the Father's right hand. See First Timothy 2:5.

Now, since Jesus has conquered death, hell and the grave (and every devil and demon who once had authority there) we are in the position of an occupation force in what was once enemy territory (see Luke 4:6).

> *Then you will make your way prosperous, and then you will have good success.*

But even a defeated enemy can practice psychological warfare. Other than that he has no weapon (see Isaiah 54:17). Oh, he can fire darts but they're not harmful (unless you receive them). And they are only fired at your mind and your tongue.[88] So with your shield of faith in place (and the rest of God's armor) you can reject (quench) all that comes against you. He has no power of his own; only the influence on your mind (thoughts) and the thoughts of others. So when people seem to be your enemy it's only because you're being influenced to enter into strife or they are. In either case reject it and stand in the liberty wherewith Christ has made you free.[89]

Do you begin to understand why 'Love' is the Royal Law?

---

[88] They're fired at your mind but his ultimate target is your tongue. If he can convince you that his lies are true and then convince you to speak his words then the way is open for him to begin to bring to pass what you have said. The process is the same (but the words are different) with your Heavenly Father. Take heed what you hear and put a watch on your mouth.

[89] Galatians 5:1

That's who Jesus is. That is the <u>knowledge of the Son of God</u>.

6) "...unto a perfect man..."

> **The level of importance and priority you give to the Word of God, and your commitment to do what it says are your recipe and guarantee of spiritual growth.**

This is where the knowledge of the Son of God leads us.

James tells us, "...My brethren, count it all joy when you fall into various trials, knowing that the testing of your faith produces patience. But let patience have its perfect work, that you may be perfect and complete, lacking nothing."[90]

Isn't it interesting how joy, faith, patience and perfection all work together. It's all about being perfect...which you and I already are. Now just have patience while your soul (mind, will and emotions) and body (flesh) get in line with your spirit.[91] Which does not mean parading around with a too-happy, not-so-bright look on your face repeating innocuous lines like, "Isn't everything wonderful!" with your teeth and fists clenched. It means finding out what the Word says about living the victorious Kingdom life, in the midst of your situation (circumstances). And then meditating on and studying that Word keeping it in your mouth and heart and before your eyes. And then doing it.

How's that 'Love' practice working out by the way. You remember, *"I" do not behave rudely, "I" do not seek my own, "I" am not provoked, "I" think no evil; "I" do not rejoice in*

---

[90] James 1:4

[91] As indicated before, the tongue is the main element by which these come into alignment. Our words are important. See Hebrews 5:12-13.

iniquity, but "I" rejoice in the truth;"I" bear all things..." etc. It's a 60-second exercise that could change your life. Go back and re-read that section if you missed it (about 10 pages back).

And while we're on the subject, here's another tip that not only works toward aligning yourself (and your circumstances) with God's will but creates meaningful (even eternal) conversation out of routine and meaningless greetings and small talk.

When asked how you are, respond with what the Word says, or at least something glowing and uplifting (edifying). Then when asked "why" or "how come you always say that" simply

> *In the meantime believe God for your needs to be met supernaturally. beginning with getting out of debt.*

respond, "This book I read says you are (or 'get') what you say. If you've done this all right someone will ask, "what book". When you say, "The New Testament", and as their eyes roll you have an opportunity to explain that it's not a religious book...it's all about life.

And you have opened the door to share the eternal truth of God's Word with another future offspring that He sacrificed His own Son for. Most folks make a real process of witnessing and sharing God's truth. But it's really very simple. Just pack a few 'conversation starters' in your bag and wait for (anticipate) the Holy Spirit to create an opening.

That's what a perfect man looks like.

7) "...unto the measure of the stature of the fullness of Christ."

One measure of the stature of the fullness of Christ is to study the phrase "in Christ" or "in Jesus" or "in Him" in the New Testament. I did; and found six pages of notes about who I already am "in Him". "So if I 'already am in Him' why do I need to study it?" Good question. And the answer is in the first verse of Hebrews chapter three. Jesus is the High Priest of what we say (profession, confession). Meaning that He is in charge of bringing to pass His Words in our mouth. In other words, when we say what His Word says (i.e., His Will) He will watch over His Word to perform it.

> **We just might not invite him back. Read some of Paul's sermons literally and see if you don't agree.**

You see, what we say without thinking about it is what has been directing our lives until now anyhow. It's just been the wrong stuff. Jesus said, *"...by our words we would be justified and by our words we would be condemned."* [92]It's true, you know. At its most fundamental level, we reject Jesus by our words. And we reverse that and receive eternal life by our words. Then He went on to say that even our idle words would be judged.[93]

So if eighty percent (or more) of our conversation is sports statistics or less than uplifting exchanges about people we don't even know (or the economy or the government) then we will not only have to answer for ourselves—but those words actually tend to order the circumstances around our lives.[94]

Notice I did not say, *"...what we say just once."* it is what we say continually that matters. And the same applies to words that we *do* want to affect our lives.

---

[92] Matthew 12:37
[93] Matthew 12:36
[94] Matthew 12:35

But how can we say what He said if we don't know it. When Joshua took over for Moses God did not tell him to pray and fast and wear special robes (all legitimate directives of the old covenant).

He told him, *"This Book of the Law shall not depart from your mouth, but you shall meditate in it day and night, that you may observe to do according to all that is written in it. For then you will make your way prosperous, and then you will have good success."* (NKJV)

> *The one who is brutally honest may in reality be more committed to the brutality than the honesty.*

So read, study and meditate on "the measure and stature of the fullness of Christ" and who you already are "in Him" and you will grow measurably in stature in Him.

[14] That we [henceforth] be no more children, tossed to and fro, and carried about with every wind of doctrine, by the sleight of men, [and] cunning craftiness, whereby they lie in wait to deceive; [15] But speaking the truth in love, may grow up into him in all things, which is the head, [even] Christ:
[Ephesians 4:14-15 KJV]

8) *"...be no more children"*

...encompasses the next two admonitions about being tossed to and fro and carried about with every wind of doctrine. In other words, grow up! Paul complained to the church at Corinth that he had many things to say but while they should be teaching others they could only bear milk and not the meat of the Word.[95]

That is at the heart of the purpose of the church. It is a thing called Spiritual Growth. And Paul explains to the folks in Galatia how to go about that.

By faith. Seriously. Read chapters two and three in Galatians. These folks thought they had to work at spiritual growth. To which Paul responded, *"Who has bewitched you?"* Pretty strong language[96] when addressing one of his church congregations. But a famous (and much misunderstood) quote from Habakkuk is found in Romans 1:17; Galatians 3:11 and Hebrews 10:38. *The just shall **live** by faith.*

> *Spiritual growth is at the core of becoming the victorious church that God intended. And growth involves change. If you haven't changed since last year then you're not growing.*

The key word here which is much misunderstood is "live". It is no different than the simple statement in Second Corinthians 5:7, *"We walk by faith and not by sight."* 'Walk' has the same intent as 'live'. Romans 1:17 became the signature verse and rallying cry of Martin Luther during the Reformation. But the revelation at that time was limited to salvation. The corrupt (and mostly godless) church leadership at the time knew nothing of 'faith'.[97] But a simple (and literal) understanding of

---

[95] 1 Corinthians 3:1-2

[96] In fact the Greek word translated "bewitched" is only found in this verse and nowhere else in the New Testament. Strong words, indeed.

[97] Don't scoff or get uppity if you're not Catholic (or offended if you are). The church leadership that went south during that regrettable time in the faith was us! This was before the reformation and *we were that church*. Both groups had their faults and both have since reformed. The call today is for UNITY and not blame.

Paul's epistles (and the words of Jesus) reveal that 'faith' *is* a way of life, not just a way to get saved.

The first few verses of Galatians chapter three make this abundantly clear. So don't worry about your spiritual growth. If your commitment is to make the Word of God final authority in your life and giving its importance first place; and finding ways to actually 'do' the Word you *will* grow. Church attendance, Bible study, prayer, fellowship with other believers, ministering to those in need and witnessing are all important elements of your life as a believer. But the level of importance and priority you give to the Word of God, and your commitment to do what it says are your recipe and guarantee of spiritual growth. Meditate on 1 Peter 5:6-7 and Matthew 11:28-30.

9) *"...tossed to and fro..."*

Our friend James again tells us to be single minded. *Let not a double minded man think that he will receive anything from the Lord*, he says. You cannot be committed to this world's system and its tenets and adhere to God's Word as well. You cannot serve two masters. Don't quit your job and start a commune in the mountains however (unless the Spirit of God tells you to). Your job and other commitments that don't seem very spiritual simply do not need to be your number one priority. The Word comes first before everything and *in* everything.

Then watch all those other areas improve. If you have His wisdom and His mind and His direction all those other areas become His priority.

So find out what God has called you to do. If it's your current occupation then work at it as unto the Lord. If not then find out where He wants you...and go there. In the meantime believe God for your needs to be met supernaturally (beginning with getting out of debt).[98] Get

---

[98] More than just a 'prosperity' concept; debt is bondage. Whatever God calls you to do (or give) is hindered by the lenders we serve. If you don't think it's servitude

involved in His Kingdom and *seek first that Kingdom and His righteousness* and those needs will be met and *all these things will be added unto you*. Now you're cooperating with His Will and His Word and His blessing will come on you and overtake you.[99]

Now share your revelation with others and the whole church will grow because of it.[100]

10) *"...carried about with every wind of doctrine..."*

Did you see that? Not all 'doctrine' is godly or biblical or even sensible.

In Acts chapter 17 Luke tells us about two churches where Paul preached. One was in Thessalonica and the other was in Berea. Paul and his friends got chased out of Thessalonica and came next to Berea and preached the same message.[101] But those in Berea were *"more noble"* because they searched the Word daily to see if those things (which Paul preached) were so.

If the Apostle Paul came to your church next week would you search the scriptures to see if he was telling the truth...and / or to root and nurture the Word sown in your heart?

My conviction is that if he did show up and were allowed to speak freely we would all be so shocked that we would not only have to check it out, we just might not invite him back.

Read some of Paul's sermons (and letters) literally and see if you don't agree. He was a Word of Faith preacher you know (Romans 10:8); with none of the usual religious trappings but with a brash kind of humility that said, *"...what you have seen in me, do"* and *"...be followers (imitators) of*

---

read the small print in your contract (covenant). Believe for freedom. See Proverbs 22:7.
[99] Deuteronomy 28:2
[100] The real goal here is to be free of the bondage of debt to the point where most or even all of your income is available for seed. And the harvest on that seed will provide a living like you've never known. Don't choke on that. Just start sowing on purpose and believing for the return (harvest) and discover for yourself that God's covenant really is true (Deuteronomy 8:18)
[101] The same message Peter preached in Acts 10:38.

me even as I am of Christ." And in three different places (that we know of) he taught the truth "*…according to my gospel.*" Here is a man who had taken ownership of the message and was not swayed by any other "*…wind of doctrine.*"

Jesus said to take heed *what* we hear and even admonished to be careful *how* we hear and with what measure. If I haven't said it already, make the Word first place and final authority in your life…and everything else will fall in line.

11) "*…speaking the truth in love…*"

What a combination! How on earth are we to do that? The truth hurts and love is cautious not to offend. That's true isn't it? Or is it?

Jesus said *the Truth will make you free.* And He also said that *the one who does not do what say does not love Me.* So truth and love work together. The important or operative word from our original statement is 'speaking'. When our words from the heart are the truth they bring forth good things according to Jesus. It only follows that when that truth is spoken in love others are blessed and even better things happen.

It has also been said that the one who is brutally honest is in reality more committed to the brutality than the honesty. If God is Love and His Word is Truth then the simple solution here is be so full of God that His Love and Truth come out in exact measure (from our spirit) without having to think about it or having to force the 'love'.

> *I know. I'm Scandinavian and not what you would call an 'extrovert'. But I have gained immeasurably from successes in this area.*

12) *"...may grow up into Him..."*

We've already talked about growing up. But apparently the Holy Spirit thought it important enough to mention twice. So be no more children, tossed to and fro and carried about with every wind of doctrine. That actually makes four times. And for good reason. Spiritual growth is at the core of becoming the victorious church that God intended.

> *What is it that you would <u>pursue</u> if time and money and success were all guaranteed and unlimited? Think about it. That's your <u>passion</u> or even your <u>calling</u>.*

One key element of spiritual growth that has not been mentioned so far is 'change'. Growth involves change. If you haven't changed since last year then you're not growing. Inertia or 'comfort' is one of the most prevalent enemies of the church. Change is uncomfortable. Your favorite sitcom; your bowling buddies; Facebook; video games; the newspaper; the TV constantly on...all become habits. Not in themselves 'bad' habits; but they are time-bandits[102] that take priority away from what is really important. And habits are hard to break. So don't break them. Create new ones.

Start with **The OnePage Solution.** It's a unique way for busy folks (especially Pastors) to allow themselves to be immersed in God's Word. Try it at ***www.TOPS.Axxiom.org***. And if you're into business planning and organization then read *The Tyranny of the Urgent* by Charles Hummel.

If you don't have time for another book then know that dealing with the 'Tyranny of the Urgent' is based on categorizing your life into four quadrants. The four quadrants are clearly shown in a graph / matrix at the end of this book.

---

[102] See 'quadrant 4' in Appendix E.

The top left is Quadrant #1. If it is both Important *and* Urgent then don't think about it. Better get 'er done. We'll come back to #2.

Quadrant #3 (urgent / not important); if it is not important then the urgency is someone else's. Get these done if you can as time allows. And Quadrant #4 (Not Urgent and Not Important). These are similar to #3 only less of a priority. Now, about #2. These are the things in your life that are *important* but *not urgent*.

This is where improving your marriage, planning for the kids' college and spiritual growth all fit (assuming your marriage is fine and your kids are still in grade school). If you were to skip everything in quadrant #2 for the next few days it probably wouldn't matter much. Which is exactly why you need to do something toward accomplishing your quadrant #2 entries at least every week. These are the things in your life that really hurt if you wait until they're urgent. So first start with creating a habit of getting into God's Word (and getting God's Word into you) and set about regular work on everything else in that little box.

If you have Spiritual growth in box #2 (and you should) then know that this is at the heart of the purpose of the church. For more on how spiritual growth is

> *But the truth is that folks do want to be involved... Encouragement to even allow themselves to be encouraged (willing to be willing) seems to be the level we need to approach.*

accomplished read the second and third chapters of Paul's letter to the Galatians.

[16] From whom the whole body fitly joined together and compacted by that which every joint supplieth, according to the effectual working in the measure of every part, maketh increase of the body unto the edifying of itself in love. [Ephesians 4:16 KJV]

13) *"...whole body fitly joined together..."*

We are all a part of the body. And we need to be in communication with the other parts. And not just on Facebook or email. Select someone of like gender whose attitude or skill or knowledge in some area you admire. Then arrange for occasional (preferably regular) meetings...in the park, the lunchroom at work, the coffee shop, etc. Their home or yours is also good but distractions like cleaning, cooking, phone and kids (not to mention your

> *Do you belong? And are you helping others to feel the same?*

spouse) can be a distraction. You should have fellowship with your spouse and your kids, too. But this is different. You need believing friends to grow with and be accountable to.

We also need an outlet to discuss matters of enduring and even eternal value. See Appendix 'F'.

Only two rules: turn off your phone, and go for understanding (listening) and not correction.

Sunday is an obvious opportunity to 'join together' with others in the body. But not for long. Most are in a hurry and conversations usually turn shallow for lack of time. Be ready with a helpful scripture (even have them printed ahead of time) or make arrangements to connect later during the week. The point is that we all need to connect and social media is only the pretense of connecting.

And be aware that no matter how desperate the need or desire to join into your 'connection attempt' others will resist. *"Pretty busy week"* or *"I'll get back with you"* or *"Sounds good I'll think about it" are fake rejections (especially if you're a guy).*
Persistence is the key…and it's worth it.[103] I know. I'm Scandinavian and not what you would call an 'extrovert' but have gained immeasurably from successes in this area.

Become a part of the body that actually pursues the benefits of 'connection'. See also Romans 12:4-5.

14) *"…every joint supplies…"*

You have a supply. You have unique talents and abilities that the body needs. And they are usually connected to what you love.

> *Know that His Word and your confession are the basic elements toward obedience. Know the Word and speak it…and hold your tongue when anything contrary comes to mind.*

What is your passion? What is it you would pursue if time and money and success were all guaranteed and unlimited? Think about it. It's probably not on the tip of your tongue. Although it could be. For most folks it's not. It takes at least a few days to overcome old patterns of thinking. Unlimited time and resources and no chance of failure are not concepts that our natural minds deal with easily. But we've been working on that, haven't we. And this is an

---

[103] Hebrews 10:24-25

extremely worthwhile exercise. Once you start to get a clear glimpse of what really moves you, you're on your way to finding out why you're here. That's your passion; and more likely than not, your calling.

Maybe you're an accountant but what you love is teaching kids to fish. Maybe you're a nurse but what you love is organizing fund-raisers or parties or other events. Or maybe you're a salesman who would love to see a bus ministry in your church.

And it doesn't have to be something so visible. We can all be prayer warriors. Find others who feel the same way and split up the list of church staff and congregation. No matter how long (or short) the list we can lay hands on the legal pad as a point of contact and agree for health, healing, salvation, spiritual growth, inspiration, deliverance, ministry, ears to hear and all seventeen points of the purpose of the church to be manifest in their lives.

15) *"...effectual working of every part..."*

The previous entry (14) was about your gifts. This one is about the gifts or participation of others.

If the church is to grow (spiritually and physically) then everyone will have to be encouraged to get involved. I know, this is just what most do not want to hear. There seems to have been an emphasis in independence and avoiding involvement in recent decades. Few of us even know who our neighbors are.

But the truth is that folks *do* want to be involved; just like in the previous point about meeting with others for the purpose of meaningful fellowship and accountability. Encouragement to even allow themselves to *be* encouraged seems to be the level we need to approach. And this seems like it would be more effective for the leadership than for the body. And certainly the church leadership can help here with some stimulus from the pulpit or in the bulletin. As an aside, the bulletin or newsletter (mostly the newsletter) can be made more effective with the congregation's input. Which provides another great opportunity for your involvement.

But while working with the staff of the church will provide inspiration and insights into their view of the purpose of the church, our point has been from the beginning that the purpose of the church is designed predominately to be carried out by the church itself (that's you and me). So we're more connected than ever to the previous two points.

A home Bible study is a good place to start if your church does not have an existing structure of 'small group' meetings. And even if they do, this is a surprising benefit to your own growth and a very effective witness and encouragement to the rest of your family. A small group or Bible study setting is a great forum for discussion of the needs of the church body and what your local church organization is in need of.

> *While he doesn't use the word 'prosper' the Holy Spirit by Paul is certainly saying that getting by...is not acceptable.*

16) *"...increase of the body..."*

Sounds like either church growth or spiritual growth. Other versions don't help here either. But connecting this with the following final statement we can only surmise that it means *both* spiritual and numerical growth. What a concept. More people coming in and those that do come in and remain are growing in the Lord. This is what the purpose of the church is all about.

. There are small churches and there are mega-churches. But we are not comparing (or shouldn't be). What matters is what is happening *in your church*. Are folks coming in and not coming back? Or do the same folks in the congregation seem stagnant in their walk with Christ? Or how about you? Do you belong? And are you helping others to feel the same? We're at the end of the seventeen points that the Apostle (and the Holy Spirit) enumerated.

So the answer to these questions are directed back to the previous points. Check yourself on each and then get to work on just a few (starting with raising the level of importance you give to God's Word). The best testimony and encouragement to others is to see the change in you. So start increasing.

> *It is obvious from these two verses as well as the ministry of Jesus and the rest of the New Testament that we have a responsibility to give...and to receive.*

17) *"...unto the edifying of itself in love."*

The conclusion takes care of itself. If we all act as if we really were part of the 'body of Christ' then success is guaranteed. With Christ as Head of the body, strife cannot enter in, divisions are non-existent, envy and gossip are stopped before they start; the church leadership is encouraged and prayed for
and the body of Christ's holy bride becomes known by those both within and without for the "...edifying of itself in love." See 1 Corinthians 14:12.

This is ultimately where the love of God leads. When we even begin to understand the love God has for us then we will live out that same love in our lives and in the church. That is God's Plan for the Church.

[17] This I say therefore, and testify in the Lord, that ye henceforth walk not as other Gentiles walk, in the vanity of their mind, [18] Having the understanding darkened, being alienated from the life of God through

the ignorance that is in them, because of the blindness of their heart: [19] Who being past feeling have given themselves over unto lasciviousness, to work all uncleanness with greediness. [Ephesians 4:17-19 KJV]

The Apostle here is referring back to his statement in chapter two, verse ten. And the 'Gentiles' there as well as here are not necessarily non-Jews. He is using the term to refer to their state before coming to know Christ to graphically contrast their previous and present condition. He is leading in to the practical application to come based on the spiritual foundation he has laid for three and one half chapters.

> *If you're in God's family then He said if you seek Him and His ways (righteousness) that He would take care of you.*

[20] But ye have not so learned Christ; [21] If so be that ye have heard him, and have been taught by him, as the truth is in Jesus: [22] That ye put off concerning the former conversation the old man, which is corrupt according to the deceitful lusts; [23] And be renewed in the spirit of your mind; [Ephesians 4:20-23 KJV]

It is Christ you have learned and it is Christ by whom you have learned. And the lesson is this: put away your old nature and renew your mind.[104]

This is no automatic process. The power, authority, ability and equipping to accomplish what He has promised is already supplied. But when He says "put off" and "be

---

[104] Follow the instructions in Romans 12:2.

renewed" then decision and action are implied. If the word picture is not clear then know that His Word and our confession are the basic elements toward obedience. Know the Word and speak it…and hold your tongue when anything contrary comes to mind.

> *Wealth, while not implying spirituality, also does not imply corruption. If it did then God is the worst one of the bunch.*

[24] And that ye put on the new man, which after God is created in righteousness and true holiness. [25] Wherefore putting away lying, speak every man truth with his neighbour: for we are members one of another. [26] Be ye angry, and sin not: let not the sun go down upon your wrath: [Ephesians 4:24-26 KJV]

And look what you're putting on. The 'new man' who is righteous and holy. You have put off what is corrupt and deceitful. Now put on the new. Speak the Truth. And lose your anger to love, forgiveness and accord. And by so doing you will give no place to the devil. All of which has to do with your words. Watch your tongue and you maintain a strong front against the enemy.

[28] Let him that stole steal no more: but rather let him labour, working with [his] hands the thing which is good, that he may have to give to him that needeth. [29] Let no corrupt communication proceed out of your mouth, but that which is good to the use of edifying, that it may minister grace unto the hearers. [30] And grieve not the holy Spirit of God, whereby ye are sealed unto the day of redemption. [31] Let all bitterness, and wrath, and anger, and clamour, and evil speaking, be put away from you, with all malice: [32] And be ye kind one to

another, tenderhearted, forgiving one another, even as
God for Christ's sake hath forgiven you.
[Ephesians 4:28-32 KJV]

Stealing on a large or small scale is still stealing. So
stop it. But the rest of the message is a powerful revelation.
Your needs (daily bread) and supply are not your own. While
he doesn't use the word
'prosper' the Holy Spirit by
Paul is certainly saying that
getting by (while the rest of the
world is in desperate need) is
not acceptable. In fact it is
selfish and disobedient.

> *One of Jesus'
> most famous
> 'giving'
> lessons
> involved a
> young rich
> guy whom he
> told to give to
> the poor.*

There are always those in
need and it is the church's job
(not the government) to supply
food, clothing, shelter,
opportunity, equipping and the
gospel to not only help but
provide a way out.[105]

Here is where the
church in its arrogance and
pride has missed a central
message of the gospel. We say we don't need a three million
dollar house but are happy to just get by with our cozy but
modest 3-2-2[106] with a small yard and white picket fence in
quiet, peaceful and safe suburbia.

What about missionaries?[107] What about the persecuted
church? What about China? What about Ecuador? What
about Israel? What about Ukraine, Iraq, Iran, Syria? And
what about the war zones of poverty in your own inner city?

---

[105] Read verse 28 again. No mention is made of his own needs...only giving to
others. Think about that.

[106] 3 bedroom, 2 bath, 2-car garage...

[107] Or 'Apostles' which simply means 'sent ones'. These committed men and
women called to do the work of Paul or Barnabas deserve better.

What about medical research? There are multitudes who don't know about (or believe in) God's healing power.

> **_Let no 'corrupting' talk come out of your mouth._**

Listen to the Holy Spirit's description of what our giving is for. *"And God is able to make all grace abound toward you; that you, always having all sufficiency in all things, may abound to every good work:"*

And in the Amplified Bible, *"And God is able to make all grace (every favor and earthly blessing) come to you in abundance; so that you may always and under all circumstances and whatever the need, be self-sufficient [possessing enough to require no aid or support and furnished in abundance for every good work and charitable donation].*[108] *(AMP)*

It is obvious from these two verses as well as the ministry of Jesus and the rest of the New Testament that we have a responsibility to give...and to receive. The receiving is for more giving as well as for your benefit. God has no problem with your enjoyment.[109] Things we enjoy (not love) only become an idol (or master) when we start thinking that *we did this.*

Think about this guy in his comfy, humble, get-by little Cape Cod style cottage. And then think about how that puts him in the top 2% of the world's economy. What hypocritical arrogant pride to say we're being humble. I'd apologize for the harshness of the language but it needs to be said and it's time someone said it.

I'm speaking of course of the economically advanced areas of the world. So if that's not where you're living then know that the same principles that prospered the United States of America will work where you live. And you don't have to change the government to enjoy the benefits. Jesus' first statement in His first sermon was addressed to the poor.

---

[108] Second Corinthians 9:8. Actually all of chapter 8 through 9:15 is worth reading / studying / meditating.

[109] John 16:24; 1 Timothy 6:17

He said that God had anointed Him to preach the gospel to the poor. Was that so they could get saved and stay poor?

Not according to His own words and actions. Jesus gave to the poor regularly and encouraged them to do the same. See Mark chapter twelve.. And He preached that if you give (even two mites) that it would be given back to you with the same measure , pressed down, shaken together and running over. In other words it makes no difference where you live or work. If you're in God's family then He said if you seek Him and His ways (righteousness) that He would take care of you.

> *"But how can I forgive when I don't feel forgiving? Besides, look what they did (said) to me."*

One brother put it this way, *"Don't work for your living. Work for your giving. Then give for your living. God will reward your giving far beyond anything any employer would be willing to pay."*

But back to the first world or whatever you call the rest of us. The poorest in our upscale western culture is still in the top 4-5% of the world's economy. And whether rich or poor, our reliance on the government has diluted our faith and even inoculated us against true belief.

So should you give to a church in an 80 acre 20 million dollar facility? Two answers. If they're preaching (and obeying) the Word, yes. Their needs and their support of missions and ministry around the world are likely more than you can imagine.

If they're not (honoring the Word), then find one that is. Neither size nor success is a measure of spiritual growth or worth. And of primary importance is God's will. Ask where you should be. And then go there.

But the point here is to give. It is the foundation of God's Kingdom economy. And not primarily to support His work. It is to support (prosper) *you.* As in Paul's example of the 'thief' that we started with, *"make what you are able and believe for the return of what you've already given so that you can not only live better but give more".* And the primary purpose of that giving is to funnel more back to you so that there will be *more* to give. If your church or other ministry is blessing and feeding you then ask God for direction and do what He says in terms of giving. If they have a big house or church or airplane then know that God knows what He's doing. And wealth, while not implying spirituality, also does not imply corruption. If it did then God is the worst one of the bunch.

Before we depart this subject let me tell you something about wealth. I mentioned a three million dollar house earlier. Did you know that if someone built a three million dollar house in your community and you and all your friends drove the evil rich guy out of town and tore his house apart...you wouldn't' find a dime in it.[110]

So where is all that money? The lumber yard, the contractor, the architect, the carpenters, the cement finishers, the furniture store, the carpet installers, the plumbers, the painters, the roofers and the bricklayers (to name a few) all have the money. And what did they do with it? Expanded their business, bought groceries, paid their car payments, gave to your church and cub scout troop. In other words the three million is right back in your community.[111]

So we need to lose the bitterness and finger pointing at success and give, not until it hurts, but until we receive our own. And lest we think that the money could have been given to the poor instead, keep in mind that anyone with that kind of income has probably given more to benefit the poor than most of us combined. Furthermore I found that when

---

[110] Except of course under the couch cushions or in the wall safe. But these have nothing to do with the $3M that you wanted to get back.

[111] Albeit some went outside, even overseas. But the local labor and suppliers (even the ones who imported from Taiwan) are the major contributors and beneficiaries of any local project.

tempted with that kind of criticism that I was quoting Judas and not Jesus.[112]

One of Jesus' most famous 'giving' lessons involved a young rich guy whom he told to give to the poor. This guy walked away grieved. But Jesus just finished telling him he would have treasure in heaven. Does that mean when he dies? No. In heaven what we call 'treasure' is used for pavement. And Jesus was not promising this guy better streets. In addition, according to Proverbs 19:17 and elsewhere what is given to the poor is paid back by God. Jesus expanded on that by saying he would not only get paid back but receive 100-fold (that's not 100 *percent*, that's 100 *times*)...now in this time! See Mark 10:29-30.

We are commanded to rejoice with those who rejoice, and weep with those who weep (Romans 12:15). But we seem in the church to weep more freely over troubles than to rejoice over someone else's success. And if that is true of you or me we will find it more difficult to do our own receiving. We need to watch our attitudes and our (corrupting) words.

The first statement in verse 29 (*Let no corrupt communication proceed out of your mouth*) is critical to our walk in the Spirit. But because the translators didn't pick up on the implication of the phrase (or the word translated 'corrupt') it comes across (and even translated that way by some) as 'profanity' or just ugly talk. But the other five times this word is used in the New Testament they are all by Jesus[113] and all refer to words spoken that contradict good fruit (or God's blessing). James refers to this kind of language as 'lying against the truth'.[114]

The English Standard Version gets it the closest (*Let no corrupting talk come out of your mouth.*) and at least gives the sense of words or conversation that 'corrupts'. This is more meaningful than "*is* corrupt" ('corrupt' is bad enough,

---

[112] John 12:4-6
[113] Matthew 7:17, 18; 12:33; 13:48; Luke 6:43
[114] James 3:14

but 'corrupting' is going to bring results you don't want) . In other words, since Jesus is the High Priest of our confession then in order for Him to minister blessing, healing, salvation or anything else in line with God's will (Word) then 'corrupting' or contrary words disconnect us from that ministry. So let your words minister grace and don't grieve the Holy Spirit by saying anything contrary to God's Word. It takes practice. But it's worth it.

> *His point is that we blaspheme the cross of Christ by letting our flesh rule.*

Again in verse 31 we are reminded to avoid evil speaking.[115] Any promise or admonition that is repeated is worth paying attention to.

When you do speak avoid bitterness and wrath and unforgiveness. *"But how can I forgive when I don't feel forgiving? Besides, look what they did (said about) to me."* Well, first of all don't wait for the feeling. Remember that the just shall *live* by faith (which is often contrary to feelings). Not just once in a while, but *"live"*

Now forgive. Whether you feel like it or not. Honoring God's Word when our feelings are contrary, God considers a high level of obedience.[116] Besides your sins were washed away (forgiven) at the cross and Jesus (according to Mark 14:36) certainly didn't feel like it.

And secondly, fault is not at issue here. Right standing with God is. So don't argue your case or try to plea bargain with God Forgive even if you're right—maybe *especially* if you're right.

And furthermore none of us will get anywhere with God while unforgiveness in our hearts. Read Mark 11:22-25.

Live God's Love in the church...and everywhere else.

---

[115] Evil speaking is simply unbelief according to Hebrews 3:12

[116] The Holy Spirit calls living above your feelings, "walking by faith and not by sight" (our physical senses). If you want to diligently seek Him then give your spirit authority over your flesh (2 Corinthians 10:3-5; Hebrews 11:6).

**[1] Be ye therefore followers of God, as dear children; [2] And walk in love, as Christ also hath loved us, and hath given himself for us an offering and a sacrifice to God for a sweetsmelling savour.
[Ephesians 5:1-2 KJV]**

These two verses may well revolutionize your understanding of scripture if you take them literally. God is a literalist, you know. I took license to refer to Jesus as an extreme, exacting literalist, while preaching one Palm Sunday. He presented Himself as King exactly 173,880 days after the command went forth to rebuild the wall and the city (Jerusalem) exactly as Daniel predicted. That's pretty exact...and literal.

Let me show you what I mean. The first verse says to be a 'follower'. But the Greek word here is *"mimētēs"* from which we get our word 'mimic'. The Amplified Version puts it this way, *"Therefore be imitators of God (copy Him and follow His example) as well-beloved children imitate their father."* (AMP)

> *It is a wake up call, accompanied by the slap of the instructor's ruler on the desk. Pay attention! Reflect on all that has been said. This is God's Word to you. Yes, you! Listen up! Christ is giving you light.*

And the next verse expands on that command. <u>Walk in the love of God</u> <u>according to the same love that He has given (put inside) you</u>.[117] Read John chapter seventeen.

And when you that the Father not only wants you to imitate Him but has Blessed you with the ability, equipment and example to do just that, then the rest of this chapter will become an encouragement rather than an admonition. See John chapter fourteen.

[3] But fornication, and all uncleanness, or covetousness, let it not be once named among you, as becometh saints; [4] Neither filthiness, nor foolish talking, nor jesting, which are not convenient: but rather giving of thanks. [5] For this ye know, that no whoremonger, nor unclean person, nor covetous man, who is an idolater, hath any inheritance in the kingdom of Christ and of God. [6] Let no man deceive you with vain words: for because of these things cometh the wrath of God upon the children of disobedience. [7] Be not ye therefore partakers with them. [Ephesians 5:3-7 KJV]

> *Submitting yourselves one to another in the fear of God.*

Fornication in both testaments refers of course to sexual sin but also often refers to idolatry; which is allowing anything to usurp God's place of priority. Avoid this trap by controlling the tongue. Notice how many times 'words' come into his admonition. Guard your tongue according to James chapters 1-3[118] and the rest of that stuff won't have a chance.

[8] For ye were sometimes darkness, but now [are ye] light in the Lord: walk as children of light: [9] (For the fruit of the Spirit [is] in all goodness and

---

[117] Ephesians 5:2 (AMP)
[118] See also Proverbs 18:21; Matthew 12:33-37

righteousness and truth;) [10] Proving what is acceptable unto the Lord. [Ephesians 5:8-10 KJV]

The Holy Spirit by Paul again reminds us where we came from and where we should be headed. The fruit of the Spirit is not for the Holy Spirit. It is for you and me…in all goodness and righteousness and truth. And the gifts of His Spirit will prove in us what is acceptable (His will) in our lives. See Romans 12:1-2.

In fact let's look at that. *"I beseech you therefore, brethren, by the mercies of God, that ye present your bodies a living sacrifice, holy, acceptable unto God, which is your reasonable service. And be not conformed to this world: but be ye transformed by the renewing of your mind, that ye may prove what is that good, and acceptable, and perfect, will of God." (KJV)*

This is just a more thorough presentation of what the Spirit is saying through these last few verses in Ephesians. But why would we sacrifice our bodies? In his letter to the Galatians Paul speaks of being 'crucified with Christ'.

And the answer in that passage (Galatians 2:20-21) can be summed up in two lines: 1) the life I now live in the flesh I live by the faith of the Son of God, and 2) I do not frustrate the grace of God.

He goes on to define 'frustrating' God's grace. It is to claim (or believe, or live as if) righteousness comes by the law (or good deeds, or works of the flesh) then Christ died for nothing.

One of the strongest statements in all of Scripture. His actual closing phrase is hard to even utter (or write), *"...then Christ is dead in vain."* These caustic, even blasphemous words set the stage for more of the Apostle's scathing words in the next verse (3:1) that we discussed earlier, *"Who has bewitched you…"*

His point is that we blaspheme the cross of Christ by letting our flesh rule. It must be crucified. The life of Christ then ascends the throne and ushers in the 'abundant' life that Jesus prophesied and then purchased at Calvary. _"It is finished"_ means nothing if we say there is yet more I must do. Accept all that your Savior accomplished. We can add nothing to it.

[11] And have no fellowship with the unfruitful works of darkness, but rather reprove [them]. [12] For it is a shame even to speak of those things which are done of them in secret. [Ephesians 5:11-12 KJV]

Again, with a clear revelation of who you are in Christ and that you are no longer your own. Walk in the presence and power and anointing of the Holy Spirit with all boldness for the love which God has shown in His Son for you. And with that love in you stand against all the evil influence around you. Trust wholly in Him knowing that you can do nothing of yourself—but able to do _"…all things through Christ which strengthens me."_

[13] But all things that are reproved are made manifest by the light: for whatsoever doth make manifest is light. [14] Wherefore he saith, Awake thou that sleepest, and arise from the dead, and Christ shall give thee light. [Ephesians 5:13-14 KJV]

We are all children of the light. And the spirit of wisdom and revelation is at work in us and revealing to those of us who have ears to hear, _"Awake…and arise from the dead, and Christ shall give thee light."_

Verse fourteen begins with 'wherefore'. And that means that what came before has led up to this point. Of course that refers to verse thirteen but by the Spirit it looks back to all we have seen since receiving the spirit of wisdom and revelation in chapter one.

It is a wake up call—accompanied by the slap of the instructor's ruler on the desk. Pay attention! Reflect on all that has been said. This is God's Word to you. Yes, you! Listen up! Christ is giving you light. Make a quality decision to meditate on those few verses this week. Write them out on a card and carry it with you to look at during lunch or at the office or between classes or when the kids finally take a nap...you get the idea.

[15] See then that ye walk circumspectly, not as fools, but as wise, [16] Redeeming the time, because the days are evil. [17] Wherefore be ye not unwise, but understanding what the will of the Lord [is]. [18] And be not drunk with wine, wherein is excess; but be filled with the Spirit; [19] Speaking to yourselves in psalms and hymns and spiritual songs, singing and making melody in your heart to the Lord; [20] Giving thanks always for all things unto God and the Father in the name of our Lord Jesus Christ; [21] Submitting yourselves one to another in the fear of God. [Ephesians 5:15-21 KJV]

Having waked us up we now have more instruction in what our flesh should look like as we walk in the Spirit.

The key verse is seventeen. *"Wherefore be ye not unwise, but understanding what the will of the Lord is."* This is the third time this subject has come up so it must be important. The will of God is not unknown. At least not to those who would be wise. And 'wisdom' according to Jesus is synonymous with the Word of God.[119] So if I haven't said it before, know that God's Word must be your number one priority if you are in the least interested in knowing the will of God in your life.

And if you have come this far then I know that you are way more than the 'least interested'. So find a way to increase your Word level…in both quantity and quality. If you haven't looked at **The OnePage Solution**[120] (it's free) then take a look and try it for sixty days (it usually takes 2-3 weeks just to get used to it) and see if it doesn't change everything.

---

[119] Luke 11:49
[120] www.TOPS.Axxiom.org

Next, verse 21 gives an introduction to the next section. In fact the next section can be summarized in that one verse.

"Submitting yourselves one to another in the fear of God."

God's message to the Church is the longest section in Paul's letter to the Ephesians and deserves a further look. So go back and review either in this book or in your Bible (Ephesians 4:1 – 5:21) and get a revelation of what God's Plan for the Church means to the Church...or more importantly to you.

CHAPTER FIVE

GOD'S PLAN FOR THE FAMILY

[15] See then that ye walk circumspectly, not as fools, but as wise, [16] Redeeming the time, because the days are evil. [17] Wherefore be ye not unwise, but understanding what the will of the Lord [is]. [18] And be not drunk with wine, wherein is excess; but be filled with the Spirit; [19] Speaking to yourselves in psalms and hymns and spiritual songs, singing and making melody in your heart to the Lord;

> *Submitting yourselves one to another in the fear of God.*

[20] Giving thanks always for all things unto God and the Father in the name of our Lord Jesus Christ; [21] Submitting yourselves one to another in the fear of God. [Ephesians 5:15-21 KJV]

Yes, you're right. We did just cover this section at the end of Chapter Four. And, yes Chapter Four of Ephesians ended 21 verses ago. But chapter divisions were put in later and they were not in the original (Paul did not write in 'chapters'). In addition this passage is a fitting conclusion to 'God's Plan for the Church' and a fitting introduction to "God's Plan for the Family'.

If families functioned according to these seven verses then discipline problems and divorce would be nonexistent.

But if we are to submit to one another then why do we hear so much controversy about husbands and (mostly) wives submitting?

Well, you may be pleased (or disappointed) to know that I have no intention of going there...except to say that of the twelve verses devoted to the subject of submission, nine are directed to husbands while only three are addressed to wives. But I do have some Scriptural insight and revelation about understanding this or any other easily debated passage...right after I quote the easily debated passage in question:

[22] Wives, submit yourselves unto your own husbands, as unto the Lord. [23] For the husband is the head of the wife, even as Christ is the head of the church: and he is the saviour of the body. [24] Therefore as the church is subject unto Christ, so [let] the wives [be] to their own husbands in every thing. [25] Husbands, love your wives, even as Christ also loved the church, and gave himself for it; [26] That he might sanctify and cleanse it with the washing of water by the word, [27] That he might present it to himself a glorious church, not having spot, or wrinkle, or any such thing; but that it should be holy and without blemish. [28] So ought men to love their wives as their own bodies. He that loveth his wife loveth himself. [29] For no man ever yet hated his own flesh; but nourisheth and cherisheth it, even as the Lord the church:

Similarly when husbands start noticing flaws in the complete Scriptural obedience of wives, or vice versa... someone's going to get run over.

[30] For we are members of his body, of his flesh, and of his bones. [31] For this cause shall a man leave his father and mother, and shall be joined unto his wife, and they two shall be one flesh. [32] This is a great mystery: but I speak concerning Christ and the church. [33] Nevertheless let every one of you in particular so love

his wife even as himself; and the wife [see] that she reverence [her] husband. [Ephesians 5:22-33 KJV]

Rule # 1: Avoid strife.[121]

You see, the instruction about and for wives is given to wives. Instruction about and for husbands is given to husbands. This section goes through chapter six, verse nine. And what I am about to say applies all the way through.

Rule # 2. What Jesus said to someone else is none of your business.[122]

If a pedestrian interested in safe conduct while navigating the downtown streets of New York, studies carefully the vehicle operator's manual he will discover for instance that it is the responsibility of the driver to avoid pedestrians at all cost. And if a driver in that same city studies the pedestrian's safety manual he will discover that pedestrians should avoid moving vehicles at all cost.

Find out what applies to you in this passage and do it. If you still feel the need to advise and enforce this passage on others then go back and read Rules #1-3

You can easily see the problems each is about to encounter. The rules (commandments) are equally true. But it is not the job of the pedestrian to enforce the vehicle operator's rules, or even act as if every vehicle operator will —or even can—obey all that is written. Nor is it the job of the driver to enforce the pedestrian's rules.

---

[121] 2 Timothy 2:23
[122] John 21:20-23

Similarly when husbands start noticing flaws in the complete Scriptural obedience of wives, or vice versa... someone's going to get run over.

Yes, Paul and Peter both had very strong words for husbands and wives. But if we read one another's rules and seek to advise or even enforce what we think, we are taking the place of the Holy Spirit and we don't qualify for that position.

Rule # 3: Forgive those who don't understand.

So, wives don't try to quantify or judge your husband's love for you as compared to how Christ loved the church and gave Himself for her.[123] And fathers don't use scripture as a lever to get your children to obey. And employers don't try to extract a better work ethic from a known (professing) Christian employee. That's not what this passage is about and we're treading on dangerous ground if we think we have that kind of latitude and authority.

Find out what the Word says to *you* and do it (whether you feel like it or not). And don't question anyone else's level of obedience. And if anyone questions your level of obedience then tell them you are instructed to love, and *"I love you. Now let's talk about the love God has for us."* Now that's aggressive forgiveness. And if they pursue the 'submission' issue then refer them to verse 21 and bless them as you walk away.

Paul told Timothy to avoid questions that gender strife...like the *'whose-wife-shall-she-be-in-heaven[124]* ploy of the Sadducees, and almost every question that has ever arisen from Ephesians chapter five.

Obey Paul's instruction and Jesus' admonition and strife within our families and the church will disappear.

[1] Children, obey your parents in the Lord: for this is right. [2] Honour thy father and mother; (which is the first commandment with promise;) [3] That it may be

---

[123] The best resource I have ever read on the subject is now a classic, The Five Love Languages by Gary Chapman. Or go to www.5LoveLanguages.com.
[124] Paul's instruction; 1 Timothy 6:4; 2 Timothy 2:23; Titus 3:9. And Jesus' discussion with the Sadducees; Matthew 22; Mark 12; Luke 20.

well with thee, and thou mayest live long on the earth. [4] And, ye fathers, provoke not your children to wrath: but bring them up in the nurture and admonition of the Lord. [5] Servants, be obedient to them that are [your] masters according to the flesh, with fear and trembling, in singleness of your heart, as unto Christ; [6] Not with eyeservice, as menpleasers; but as the servants of Christ, doing the will of God from the heart; [7] With good will doing service, as to the Lord, and not to men: [8] Knowing that whatsoever good thing any man doeth, the same shall he receive of the Lord, whether [he be] bond or free. [9] And, ye masters, do the same things unto them, forbearing threatening: knowing that your Master also is in heaven; neither is there respect of persons with him. [Ephesians 6:1-9 KJV]

Find out what applies to *you* in this passage and do it. If you still feel you need to advise and enforce this passage on others then go back and read Rules number 1 - 3.

CHAPTER SIX

GOD'S PLAN FOR VICTORY

[10] Finally, my brethren, be strong in the Lord, and in the power of his might. [11] Put on the whole armour of God, that ye may be able to stand against the wiles of the devil. [12] For we wrestle not against flesh and blood, but against principalities, against powers, against the rulers of the darkness of this world, against spiritual wickedness in high [places]. [13] Wherefore take unto you the whole armour of God, that ye may be able to withstand in the evil day, and having done all, to stand. [Ephesians 6:10-13 KJV]

Finally is right! Paul's conclusion to this excursion through the heavenlies is—along with 2 Corinthians 10:3-5—the most powerful frontal attack on the enemy and his minions in all of scripture.

Strong words but true. Entire chapters in Genesis, Exodus, Joshua, 1st and 2nd Kings, etc. can be cited as battle plans but none so succinct nor packed with God's burden-removing, yoke destroying power than these.

> *Be strong in the LORD and in the power of His might.*

God had me quoting and then memorizing both of these passages some time back while in the midst of some pretty extreme warfare…which of course our side won. But the real life changer came later when He instructed me to keep these words alive by standing on them during the 'good' times. This I have done since, and no serious (or at least long-lasting) attack has been able to stand against God's armor and battle plan.

So let's look at it.

First of all be strong. But not in your own strength. *"In the Lord and in the power of His might."* This is God's Word, you understand. And what He commands He also authorizes and equips to carry out. So this is no small request or salutation as we march off to battle. God according to Romans 4:17 calls those things that be not as though they were. And He gets everything He says. So when He says *"Be strong"* it is no different than Him saying *"Light be"* and light was. In other words if He tells you and me to be strong —we are.

> **In other words something must be done with what you know.**

And it is faith that converts God's Word into power So gather up your faith and see the next step in God's battle plan.

The next step after receiving God's strength and mighty power is to understand who we're fighting.

Our battle (already won by the way) is not with our boss or neighbor or unbelieving brother in law. Our battle is with the real enemy; the one who brings strife and trouble through those he can influence. This may come as a surprise to you but our enemy has no power. He cannot do a thing against you that you do not receive. in fact he cannot even operate in this earth without the use of one who has authority here. If he can't find someone through whom to annoy (or even persecute) you or get you to act on the hideous thoughts he's putting in your head, then he can do nothing.

So the armor of God has two purposes. First to protect you from the enemy's influence (defense). And second to equip you to attack and keep him out of your affairs so that influence can't even get close (offense).

That is what the Apostle means when he says we wrestle not against flesh and blood. Our real enemy consists of principalities and powers and rulers and spiritual hosts. Sounds daunting, I know. But that's why I explained first that he is powerless. However his military structure remains (until cast into the lake of fire). And he will use that structure to make us believe his lies.

"But if I'm a believer then how come my kid's get sick?"

Unfortunately being a believer (alone) doesn't protect anything, any more than being friends (or even family) with the people at the alarm system company will keep you safe from being robbed. It is the believer's responsibility to find out his rights and privileges and then act on them according to God's instruction (commandments, wisdom). In other words something must be done with what you know. Like actually calling the alarm company, arranging the

That's why you can put on God's Breastplate. If you were not righteous He certainly would not let you wear it.

installation, finding out how it operates, and then turning it on —maybe even keeping it on. Get the idea? For more help on accessing your rights, privileges, weapons, and authority see Appendix 'D' at the end of the book.

Meanwhile we are reminded a second time to take the whole armor…not just part. If we're going to stand in this evil day we're going to need it…all.

[14] Stand therefore, having your loins girt about with truth, and having on the breastplate of righteousness; [15] And your feet shod with the preparation of the gospel of peace; [Ephesians 6:14-15 KJV]

Stand. Once more an important command is repeated. We are reminded not to ever let down our guard.

And to take on first the girdle (or weapons belt) of truth. Jesus said God's Word is truth…as does the book of Proverbs and the 138th Psalm. And the longest chapter in the Bible, Psalm 119 tells us of the value and importance of God's truth (His Word) in each of its 176 verses.[125]

> *Almost everything you could ever want is a part of that salvation. It also includes peace, healing, wholeness and deliverance*

Take God's Word first. Give it first place in your life, your faith, your family, your marriage, your business (job, career), your future…every area of your life…put His Word first.

****

And put on the breastplate of righteousness. Did you even know that you were righteous? It's true. That's why you can put on God's breastplate.[126]

If you were not righteous He certainly wouldn't let you wear it.

"But I sure don't feel righteous."

That may be so, but according to Second Corinthians 5:17-21 if you're a born-again Spirit-filled child of God, you have been made the very righteousness of God in Christ. Read that passage a few times then tape it to your fridge or bathroom mirror and read it again every day until it soaks in.

Righteousness is not perfection.

We should be growing closer to God every day…and improving in our conduct and conversation. But

---

[125] A unique project has been recently completed by the author which restructures Psalm 119, which is in an 'acrostic' literary form (every eight verses begin with a successive letter of the Hebrew alphabet) into an English acrostic. It is now available at no charge for a limited time. That means that you can enjoy the same memory and study helps as well as the beauty and unique literary style of the ancient Hebrews. Go to SLVCC.org/free-gift to receive your copy.

[126] Second Corinthians 5:17-21

righteousness means right standing with God.
Righteousness means that we have the authority to come before the throne of God boldly…as if we belonged—we do. So put on His breastplate.

One of the most exquisite passages in all of scripture is found in Isaiah 52:7:

How beautiful upon the mountains
Are the <u>feet of him</u>
Who brings good news,
Who <u>proclaims peace</u>,
Who brings glad tidings of good things,
Who proclaims salvation,
Who says to Zion,
"Your God reigns!"

If you can find the song that has been made of this passage you will be even more blessed. This is the verse and concept that the Spirit of God is bringing to light when He says to have your feet shod with the gospel of peace. The Gospel is the power of God unto salvation. And 'Peace' is part of salvation. In fact almost everything you could ever want is a part of that salvation. Look the word up in your concordance. It includes peace, healing, wholeness and deliverance as well as salvation.[127] Preach peace. It is what the world so desperately needs.

> *Apparently the Shield of Faith is extremely important.*

[16] Above all, taking the shield of faith, wherewith ye shall be able to quench all the fiery darts of the wicked. [17] And take the helmet of salvation, and the

---

[127] See the first page of Chapter 1 for more detail.

sword of the Spirit, which is the word of God:
[Ephesians 6:16-17 KJV]

Verse sixteen is interesting. First he says 'above all'. Then take the shield of faith. And then he tells us what it will do for us, "quench all the fiery darts of the enemy". Apparently the shield of faith is extremely important. Every Roman soldier understood the importance of his shield. All the rest of his equipment is passive, stationary.[128] But the shield is his main defensive weapon. He can position it where it will do the most good. So he must learn to be skillful in its use.

> ### *Have you ever been so 'smitten' that you jumped every time the phone rang?*

Our shield is our faith. And it is our main defensive weapon against the enemy. Learn how to use it. Practice its use until it becomes second nature. All the fiery darts of the enemy are directed at your mind and your tongue. Protect both with the shield of faith…above all.[129]

****

The helmet of salvation includes everything previously mentioned on the subject. It is the critical protection from a deadly wound. If there is any question whether your helmet is man made (religious or moral traditions) or God's own armor (containing the very life of God himself) then don't go without it another hour. Page fifteen of this book contains instruction on how to make sure you have the right (heavenly issue) helmet. Turn there with all your heart and then come back and continue being equipped with God's own armor and not some import. Put on the helmet of salvation.

---

[128] Except his sword which we will address shortly.
[129] 2 Corinthians 10:3-5; Proverbs 18:21 (especially vs. 5)

****

The only offensive weapon listed (or needed…other than prayer) is the sword of the Spirit…which is the Word of God. *"But I thought the belt of truth was the Word of God."* You thought right. There are two words used for God's 'Word' in the Greek. One is '*logos*' and the other is '*rhema*'. '*Logos*' is typically used when referring to the written word and '*rhema*' is typically used of the spoken word.

In the context of this passage, the Word that you wear is the Word you hear (or take in daily through study, reading, meditation, hearing Bible preaching and sharing with others). Study the phrase, *"have ears to hear"* or the word '*hearken*' (KJV) to know more.

> *Prayer is not always included in descriptions of God's armor. But without it nothing works.*

The sword on the other hand is wielded as needed. It is the Word you speak in direct attack against the enemy. The Word you planted in your spirit is what makes this weapon sharp. According to Hebrews 4:12-16 it is also two-edged and unstoppable.

The clearest illustration of this Sword of the Spirit's use is Jesus' example when confronted by the enemy at the very outset of His ministry. In the fourth chapters of both Matthew and Luke[130] the deployment of God's Word is shown to be the ultimate weapon against the enemy's attacks. What is also important to note is that three confrontations are recorded. The first two Jesus cast down with the 'logos', *"It is written…"* and the third with 'rhema', *"it is said…"* In any case the Word accomplished that for which it was sent.

---

[130] In fact the heart of both these passages is found in verse four (Matthew 4:4; Luke 4:4). *Man shall…live by every Word that proceeds from the mouth of God.*

Wear (hear) the Word and wield (bear) the Sword.

[18] Praying always with all prayer and supplication in the Spirit, and watching thereunto with all perseverance and supplication for all saints; [Ephesians 6:18 KJV]

Prayer is not always included in descriptions of God's armor. But without it nothing works. Prayer is your access to your Commander in Chief. It is where your orders come from. Pray in the Spirit. Pray in the understanding.

> *That I may open my mouth boldly to make known the mystery of the Gospel...that in it I may speak boldly as I ought to speak.*

Pray with supplication and watching and perseverance. But pray. Practice and study all the weapons of our warfare. Become skillful in their use. But start by becoming skillful in prayer. Not just learning all the right (Elizabethan English) words to say[131]. But coming boldly before the throne of grace to obtain mercy and grace to help in time of need. In other words...as if you belonged... *you do.*

Have you ever been so 'smitten' that you jumped every time the phone rang because it just might be the one?

Well, that is just the way your Heavenly Father feels when we finally get around to talk to Him. If you don't believe that then go back and read chapters one through three. Pick up the phone sometime just to ask what He's thinking about. He just might surprise you with something from the spirit of wisdom and revelation that will revolutionize your life. He really is waiting by the phone. And the number of His direct line is Jeremiah 33:3.

---

[131] God doesn't speak Elizabethan English. So get real. He knows who you are and what you've done. And yes, He still loves you...always has...always will.

[19] And for me, that utterance may be given unto me, that I may open my mouth boldly, to make known the mystery of the gospel, [20] For which I am an ambassador in bonds: that therein I may speak boldly, as I ought to speak. [21] But that ye also may know my affairs, [and] how I do, Tychicus, a beloved brother and faithful minister in the Lord, shall make known to you all things: [22] Whom I have sent unto you for the same purpose, that ye might know our affairs, and [that] he might comfort your hearts. [23] Peace [be] to the brethren, and love with faith, from God the Father and the Lord Jesus Christ. [24] Grace [be] with all them that love our Lord Jesus Christ in sincerity. Amen. [Ephesians 6:19-24 KJV]

"And for me". While we're on the subject of prayer, pray this one for yourself. Read verses 19 and 20 and personalize it. Make the 'me' 'you'. *"...that I may open my mouth boldly to make known the mystery of the gospel."*

"Oh I could never do that."

Why not? Read the fourth chapter of Acts. Did you know that the boldness that turned the world upside down after their prayer meeting didn't come by accident? It came because they prayed for it.

And finally receive verses 23 and 24 personally...just like we did at the beginning of this journey with verse two in the first chapter.

Peace, love and grace be *to you* from God the Father and our Lord Jesus Christ with all them that love our Lord Jesus Christ in sincerity.

Amen.

CHAPTER SEVEN
CONCLUSION

What is "**God's Prayer for Us**?"

[17] that the God of our Lord Jesus Christ, the Father of glory, may give to you the <u>spirit of wisdom and revelation</u> in the knowledge of Him, [18] the <u>eyes of your understanding being enlightened</u>; that you may know what is the hope of His calling, what are the riches of the glory of His inheritance in the saints, [19] and <u>what [is] the exceeding greatness of His power toward us who believe, according to the working of His mighty power</u> [20] <u>which He worked in Christ when He raised Him from the dead</u> and seated [Him] at His right hand in the heavenly [places], [21] <u>far above all principality and power and might and dominion, and every name that is named, not only in this age but also in that which is to come</u>. [22] And He put all [things] under His feet, and gave Him [to be] head over all [things] to the church, [23] <u>which is His body</u>, the fullness of Him who fills all in all.
[Ephesians 1:17-23 NKJV]

...and "**God's Bragging Rights**?"

[4] But God, who is <u>rich in mercy</u>, because of His <u>great love with which He loved us</u>, [5] even when we were dead in trespasses, <u>made us alive</u> together with Christ (by grace you have been saved), [6] and <u>raised [us] up</u> together, and made [us] <u>sit together</u> in the heavenly [places] in Christ Jesus, [7] <u>that in the ages to come He might show the exceeding riches of His grace in [His] kindness toward us</u> in Christ Jesus. [Ephesians 2:4-7 NKJV]

...and "**God's Love Without Limits**?"

[16] that He would grant you, according to the riches of His glory, to be strengthened with might through His Spirit in the

inner man, [17] that _Christ may dwell in your hearts through faith_; that you, being rooted and grounded in love, [18] may be _able to comprehend with all the saints what [is] the width and length and depth and height_-- [19] _to know the love of Christ which passes knowledge_; that you may be _filled with all the fullness of God._ [20] Now to Him who is able to do _exceedingly abundantly above all that we ask or think_, according to the _power that works in us_,
[Ephesians 3:16-20 NKJV]

...and "**God's Plan for the Church**?"

[12] ...the _perfecting of the saints_, for the _work of the ministry_, for the _edifying of the body of Christ_: [13] Till we all come in the _unity of the faith_, and of the _knowledge of the Son of God_, unto a perfect man, unto the measure of the stature of the fulness of Christ: [14] That we henceforth be _no more children_, tossed to and fro, and carried about with every wind of doctrine, by the sleight of men, and cunning craftiness, whereby they lie in wait to deceive; [15] But _speaking the truth in love_, may _grow up_ into him in all things, which is the head, even Christ: [Ephesians 4:12-15 KJV]

...and "**God's Plan for the Family**?"

[1] Be ye therefore _followers of God_, as dear children; ... [17] Wherefore be ye not unwise, but _understanding what the will of the Lord is_. ... [21] _Submitting yourselves one to another_ in the fear of God. [Ephesians 5:1, 17, 21 KJV]

...and "**God's Plan for Victory**?"

[10] Finally, my brethren, _be strong in the Lord_, and in the power of his might. [11] _Put on the whole armour of God_, that ye _may be able to stand_ against the wiles of the devil. ... [13] Wherefore take unto you the _whole armour of God_, that ye _may be able to withstand_ in the evil day, and having done all, to _stand_. ... [18] _Praying always_ with all prayer and supplication in the Spirit, and watching thereunto with all

perseverance and supplication for all saints; [19] And for me, that utterance may be given unto me, that I may open my mouth boldly, to make known the mystery of the gospel, [Ephesians 6:10-11, 13, 18-19 KJV]

The Love of God is eternal...and the Love of God is immeasurable...and the Love of God is undeserved and beyond imagination. But the Love of God is *not unattainable.*

What this journey has attempted to convey is that the Love of God is for you. His commandments / words are important but they are not grievous. They are designed to keep us under the cover of the BLESSING. Jesus was the Last Adam meaning that He walked in the BLESSING and authority that Adam walked in before the fall. That is what He wants (and has provided) for us.

He longs to treat us...as if sin never existed. Don't consider it robbery to receive and walk in that extravagant Love today. This is The Love of God!

APPENDIX A:

Understanding Scripture

The Father, Son and Holy Spirit are all extreme, exacting literalists.

And why not? Aren't you? Or do you have to add, *"No, I really mean it this time"* when you intend to be literal?

Jesus said for us to be literal and not cryptic.[132] So why would He be? You also know that 'testament' is another word for 'covenant', right? In other words, a blood-sworn oath, a legal and binding contact. Would you be cryptic or figurative in a legal contract? Of course not.

Here are four simple steps to understanding scripture. **1)** take it for exactly what it says. **2)** if it's obviously figurative (i.e., you are salt and light) then find the literal meaning intended by the figurative language, and **3)** if it's still unclear then pray for wisdom and revelation so that the Holy Spirit can guide you into all truth.[133] **4)** if you didn't hear the answer then know that you will. And set the issue aside for more research later.

You may have noticed that consulting commentaries or calling everyone you know (including your pastor) were not included in the list. That's not because those options are bad. But these steps are better...or at least primary Common sense and the guidance of the Holy Spirit are the preferred method. Reserve consulting someone else's opinion as a last resort.

If it comes to that, the best 'commentary' that I have found is my Strong's Concordance. But a very close second place is the Amplified Bible. It is a word-for-word translation (similar to the KJV) but with expanded (amplified) meaning added to clarify the passage. And footnotes include extensive references for further research.

This still gets into a certain amount of commentary; but only in a limited sense. Still, Scripture is to be compared to Scripture. Use the wisdom of man sparingly.

---

[132] Matthew 5:37
[133] John 16:13

Primarily, remember this. If God wanted you (us) confused about His plan, His will and His purpose and nature, all He had to do was keep silent. But He did not. Remember that. It will help you more than a room full of commentaries.

God is certainly intelligent enough to say exactly what He means.

APPENDIX B:

Becoming skillful in the use of God's Word

Did you know that God's Word is a tool? Some folks in Hebrews chapter five were 'unskillful' in it's use. The writer by the Holy Spirit calls them 'babes'. And we are told time and again to 'grow up'. Jesus said that man lives by every Word of God. If we're living by our wits and good looks and education then we're not using the tools God gave us. You may be witty and good looking and educated—even successful—but God has a plan that *'...maketh rich and addeth no sorrow with it."*[134]

Here's how it works. *Read, study, meditate, confess...*and *do* His Word.

Keep that up for a while and you will become skillful in using and rightly discerning His Word. Consider this familiar verse, *"Trust in the LORD with all your heart and lean not to your own understanding. In all your ways acknowledge Him and He will direct your paths."*[135]

What would your life look like if the God of Creation, the God of Creativity, the Master Inventor, the All-knowing Counselor, the Parenting and Marriage Expert, the Source of All Business, Communication, Electronics, Economic and Marketing Genius...and the richest, most successful Being in all history were directing your paths?

I have been known to refer to this passage as the highest promise in all of scripture. Think about it. If He is actually directing your paths, how could you ever go wrong? Will He lead you into confusion, defeat, sickness, lack or a bad marriage? Some of course who think this is how God instructs and corrects His children would say, "Yes." But when you understand that it is His Holy Spirit that leads us into all truth and His correction (even chastisement) is from His written Word then we would have to shout a resounding, "No."

---

[134] Proverbs 10:22
[135] Proverbs 3:5-6

So find a way to get into God's Word (He calls it 'seeking Him' or His Kingdom) permanently, not for just one year.[136] You will find yourself becoming skillful in its use. And He will reward you according to His promise.[137]

[136] I refer you again to *The OnePage Solution*. Details at www.TOPS.Axxiom.org or www.SLVCC.org/free-gift.
[137] Hebrews 11:6

APPENDIX C:

Faith

Everything promised in God's Word is received by faith. It is not by chance or coincidence. Faith is God's plan for His creation. This is not to make things difficult for you and me.[138] There is good reason for His design. It is to keep what is promised to you out of the hands of the enemy.

Satan functions under only one principle—fear. He has no faith. Fear is the corrupted or twisted form of faith. He not only operates by fear, he is fear. The reason you and I are commanded to abandon fear is that fear connects us to satan. And disconnects us from the power of God.

Faith is therefore our secure connection to God and all His promises. Salvation is by faith; healing, miracles and deliverance are by faith; hearing from God and the ability to carry out His instructions are by faith. Even receiving His written Word is by faith.

But how does faith work, exactly? Where and how do we get it? How do we grow in it? And how do we use it?

In short, faith 'works' according to the same Kingdom process as any of the other gifts or fruit of His Spirit.

And we 'get it' by hearing.[139] Selective hearing, that is. Faith comes by hearing the Word of God.

And we 'grow' it by planting. According to Mark 4:14 the Word is a seed and becomes active in our lives when it is sown or planted in our hearts.

And we 'use' (or release) our faith by speaking[140] as if we believed it. And then acting on what His Word says.

The 'Kingdom process' is simply the structure that God has used from the beginning to accomplish His purpose. In the beginning...He spoke and His Spirit carried out His Words. When Jesus was on the earth He only said

---

[138] Remember Jesus' simple faith confession: "According to your faith be it unto you." and ours, "Be it unto me Sir, according to Your Word."
[139] Romans 10:17
[140] 2 Corinthians 4:13

what He heard the Father say and He only did what He saw the Father do.[141] Our instructions are to do the same.

"Faith comes by hearing..." Romans 10:17 is familiar to many. But what is hearing, actually? Well, it's continual for one thing. Kenneth Hagin is known for saying that faith does not come by *having heard*. In other words, it is not past tense. Continue to hear the Word.

But then what is hearing? It may not be what you think. Read the fourth chapter of Mark's gospel. It is all about 'hearing' the Word. Only one group in four that heard the Word (verses 3-9) actually benefited from it. Once received (heard) the enemy comes immediately to steal it.

Once planted it must be protected, watered, nurtured and cared for so that it can bring forth fruit. After hearing the Word, talk about it, meditate on it, chew on it, so to speak. Feed your spirit with the Word every day. A good measure is to spend as much time feeding on the Word as you do feeding your flesh. If this is too much of a jump at first then get at least one meal a day's worth into your spirit. If you have a good organized plan for this you will find it creates its own hunger. And you will look forward to your time planting new Word and nurturing what is already in there.

Growing your faith has already been covered above. 'Getting' and 'growing' are part of the same process. So what about 'using' your faith?

You use your faith by practice. And at the heart of that 'practice' is speaking words of faith. If you're new to this then start with the verses that we have just discussed regarding how faith works, how faith is obtained and how faith is grown. When using your faith don't start with world peace or feeding the world's hungry (unless you're studying to be Miss America). Start with paying your credit card charges at the end of the month...and eventually pay it off. You will find (surprisingly) that the reason you feel compelled to 'charge'

---

[141] John 14:10

is that your 'payments' make it 'necessary'. Then believe for doubling up on your car payment until it's paid off. In other words get out of debt (bondage)..

Now find the answer to your challenge in God's Word. (you'll find debt covered in Romans 13 and Deuteronomy 28) Write it down and confess (read) it aloud regularly until it gets down into your spirit. The Word says for faith to work it must be believed in the heart (spirit) and confessed with the mouth. Both are important.

The next step is patience. See James 1:2-4 and Hebrews 6:12 and Hebrews 10:35-36. These are all great 'faith' scriptures which should also be written down, studied, meditated on and confessed.

Patience means to be consistently constant. So hang in there. You're on your way.

This brief summary is just a beginning. But the foundation is the Word of God. So while you research more revelation about the subject of faith...always continue in the Word. You will never be the same.

SCRIPTURE REFERENCES

The sower sows the Word.   MARK 4:14 (NKJV)

6 But the righteousness of faith speaks in this way, "Do not say in your heart, 'Who will ascend into heaven?'"(that is, to bring Christ down from above) 7 or, "'Who will descend into the abyss?'" (that is, to bring Christ up from the dead). 8 But what does it say? "The word is near you, in your mouth and in your heart" (that is, the word of faith which we preach)
ROMANS 10:6-8   (NKJV)

So then faith comes by hearing, and hearing by the
Word of God.   ROMANS 10:17 (NKJV)

And since we have the same spirit of faith, according to what is written, "I believed and therefore I spoke," we also believe and therefore speak,   2 CORINTHIANS 4:13 (NKJV)

2 My brethren, count it all joy when you fall into various trials, 3 knowing that the testing of your faith produces patience. 4 But let patience have its perfect work, that you may be perfect and complete, lacking nothing.   JAMES 1:2-4   (NKJV)

9 Jesus said to him, "Have I been with you so long, and yet you have not known Me, Philip? He who has seen Me has seen the Father; so how can you say, 'Show us the Father'? 10 Do you not believe that I am in the Father, and the Father in Me? The words that I speak to you I do not speak on My own authority; but the Father who dwells in Me does the works. 11 Believe Me that I am in the Father and the Father in Me, or else believe Me for the sake of the works themselves.

12 "Most assuredly, I say to you, he who believes in Me, the works that I do he will do also; and greater works than these he will do, because I go to My Father. 13 And whatever you ask in My name, that I will do, that the Father may be glorified in the Son. 14 If you ask anything in My name, I will do it.

JOHN 14:9-14 (NKJV)

11 And we desire that each one of you show the same diligence to the full assurance of hope until the end, 12 that you do not become sluggish, but imitate those who through faith and patience inherit the promises.   HEBREWS 6:11-12

35 Therefore do not cast away your confidence, which has great reward. 36 For you have need of endurance, so that after you have done the will of God, you may receive the promise:

HEBREWS 10:35-36 (NKJV)

1 Now faith is the substance of things hoped for, the evidence of things not seen... But without faith it is impossible to please Him, for he who comes to God must believe that He is, and that He is a rewarder of those who diligently seek Him.

HEBREWS 11:1; 6 (NKJV)

3 "Listen! Behold, a sower went out to sow. 4 And it happened, as he sowed, that some seed fell by the wayside; and the birds of the air came and devoured it. 5 Some fell on stony ground, where it did not have much earth; and immediately it sprang up because it had no depth of earth. 6 But when the sun was up it was scorched, and because it had no root it withered away. 7 And some seed fell among thorns; and the thorns grew up and choked it, and it yielded no crop. 8 But other seed fell on good ground and yielded a crop that sprang up, increased and produced: some thirty-fold, some sixty, and some a hundred." 9 And He said to them, "He who has ears to hear, let him hear!"

MARK 4:3-9 (NKJV)

APPENDIX D:

Exercising your rights, privileges, authority and warfare

This sounds like a book in itself. But if you are not unskillful in the Word of Righteousness as Hebrews 5:12 or Galatians 4:1 or 1 Corinthians 3:1 tells us then a simple outline will suffice (see Appendix B if you need help). And any further clarification will come from comparing scripture with scripture in your own study.

Start with researching the phrases '*in Christ*', '*in Him*', '*in the Lord*' , '*in Whom*' and '*partakers of*' *in* the New Testament. You may be familiar with this powerful concept and may even have a list from some author of 'Who I am in Christ'. And while the list is helpful, nothing can replace your own study (having received the spirit of wisdom and revelation). So the first step in 'exercising' your rights and authority is finding out what they are.

If the extent of your understanding of your rights and privileges in Christ is getting saved then you will not even pursue healing, miracles, deliverance or the baptism of the Holy Spirit.

But Jesus said to '*seek*' His Kingdom.[142] You don't need to 'seek' what you've already found...unless there is more to know (find). And the Spirit in the book of Hebrews said to '*diligently seek*' Him.[143] And Peter reminds us to "*...grow in grace and in the knowledge of our Lord and Savior Jesus Christ.*"[144]

The next step is to say (confess, profess) who you are and with what authority and power you command what you say. The words of your mouth are important. What your spirit hears (especially from you), it believes. And since Jesus is the High Priest of our profession then for Him to fulfill His duty in that office He must have our words to work with—not our thoughts or good intentions.

---

[142] Matthew 6:33
[143] Hebrews 11:6
[144] 2 Peter 3:18

Now get specific about your privileges and your warfare. Your privileges are what you want and your warfare is for what you don't want.

Let's start with what you don't want. In Matthew chapters 16 and 18 Jesus gave us a description of how to command both the angels and evil spirits that affect our lives, *"...Whatsoever ye shall bind on earth shall be bound in heaven: and whatsoever ye shall loose on earth shall be loosed in heaven."*

'Heaven' here is better translated 'heavenlies' or 'upper atmosphere'. Nothing in God's heaven is in need of binding or loosing. The battleground of angelic forces is here on earth, or more specifically 'earth's atmosphere'. This is the 'heavenlies' where angel armies and rulers of the darkness respond to God-given words of loosing and binding.

Now understand how to communicate.

The enemy's forces are already defeated; spoiled and stripped of all the authority and power they once stole from mankind.[145] But satan is an outlaw. He is a liar and deceives the whole world according to Revelation 12:9 and John 8:44. So he's a bully. And a bully's only power is fear; or that which you give him (or allow him to have). So the only thing that matters here is knowing your position and his. Your position is in the name of Jesus and his is that he must bow the knee and flee when commanded. And like a horse knows whether its rider (master) is in control (or not), the enemy will push for all the latitude he can get. Don't give him any.[146] Bind their authority and activities and move on in faith knowing (believing in your heart) that whatsoever you say will come to pass (see Mark 11:22-23).

And the angel armies of the Creator of the universe are commissioned to <u>minister</u> for those who shall be <u>heirs of salvation</u> (see Hebrews 1:14;and Psalm 91:11-12). They

---

[145] Colossians 2:15

[146] Just like Jesus. He said that snake *"...has nothing* [no place] *in Me."* Also Ephesians 4:27

excel in strength, do His commandments and hearken to the voice of His Word (see Psalm 103:20). Knowing just this much you can loose them with boldness to accomplish anything within God's will. But set a watch over your mouth so that your words are not mixed or double minded (see Psalm 141:3 and Malachi 3:13). And move on in faith knowing (believing in your heart) that what you desired you shall have (see Mark 11:24-25).[147]

So what about your kids? Children can learn (and practice) spiritual principles at a surprisingly young age. But give them all the protection you can while they're learning. Psalm 91[148] is a good place to start. Then research every scripture that covers your family (seed) and speak what you have learned over them ...constantly. The same applies to all the other areas of your life: marriage, finances, work, church, outreach and physical and mental health.

Make your own confessions on 3x5 cards[149] and keep them in your pocket, tape them to the fridge and bathroom mirror and your cubicle at work (or file cabinet or dashboard of your truck or school notebook). *"...and the God of Peace shall be with you."* (Philippians 4:8-9).

SCRIPTURE REFERENCES

12 For though by this time you ought to be teachers, you need someone to teach you again the first principles of the oracles of God; and you have come to need milk and not solid food. 13 For everyone who partakes only of milk is unskilled in the word of righteousness, for he is a babe. 14 But solid food belongs to those who are of full age, that is, those who by reason of use have their senses exercised to discern both good and evil.
HEBREWS 5:12-14 (NKJV)

---

[147] Even if you don't see it right away (2 Corinthians 5:7). See Appendix 'C' re. Faith / Patience.

[148] Sixteen of the most powerful verses in all of scripture.

[149] Some are already included with this book. If they were omitted or have been misplaced please request a free set at our address at the front of the book.

1 And I, brethren, could not speak to you as to spiritual people but as to carnal, as to babes in Christ. 2 I fed you with milk and not with solid food; for until now you were not able to receive it, and even now you are still not able;

1 CORINTHIANS 3:1 (NKJV)

18 "Assuredly, I say to you, whatever you bind on earth will be bound in heaven, and whatever you loose on earth will be loosed in heaven. 19 "Again I say to you that if two of you agree on earth concerning anything that they ask, it will be done for them by My Father in heaven. 20 For where two or three are gathered together in My name, I am there in the midst of them."

MATTHEW 18:18-19 (NKJV)

So the great dragon was cast out, that serpent of old, called the Devil and Satan, who deceives the whole world; he was cast to the earth, and his angels were cast out with him.

REVELATION 12:9   (NKJV)

42 Jesus said to them, "If God were your Father, you would love Me, for I proceeded forth and came from God; nor have I come of Myself, but He sent Me. 43 Why do you not understand My speech? Because you are not able to listen to My word. 44 You are of your father the devil, and the desires of your father you want to do. He was a murderer from the beginning, and does not stand in the truth, because there is no truth in him. When he speaks a lie, he speaks from his own resources, for he is a liar and the father of it.

JOHN 8:42-44   (NKJV)

22 So Jesus answered and said to them, "Have faith in God. 23 For assuredly, I say to you, whoever says to this mountain, 'Be removed and be cast into the sea,' and does not doubt in his heart, but believes that those things he says will be done, he will have whatever he says. 24 Therefore I say to you, whatever things you ask when you pray, believe that you receive them, and you will have them. 25 "And whenever you stand praying, if you have anything against anyone, forgive him, that your Father in heaven may also forgive you your trespasses.

MARK 11:22-25 (NKJV)

19 And I will give you the keys of the kingdom of heaven, and whatever you bind on earth will be bound in heaven, and whatever you loose on earth will be loosed in heaven."

MATTHEW 16:19   (NKJV)

1 What I am saying is that as long as an heir is underage, he is no different from a slave, although he owns the whole estate. 2 The heir is subject to guardians and trustees until the time set by his father. 3 So also, when we were underage, we were in slavery under the elemental spiritual forces of the world. 4 But when the set time had fully come, God sent his Son, born of a woman, born under the law, 5 to redeem those under the law, that we might receive adoption to sonship. 6 Because you are his sons, God sent the Spirit of his Son into our hearts, the Spirit who calls out, "Abba, Father." 7 So you are no longer a slave, but God's child; and since you are his child, God has made you also an heir. GALATIANS 4:1-7 (NKJV)

APPENDIX E

The URGENT / IMPORTANT matrix[150]

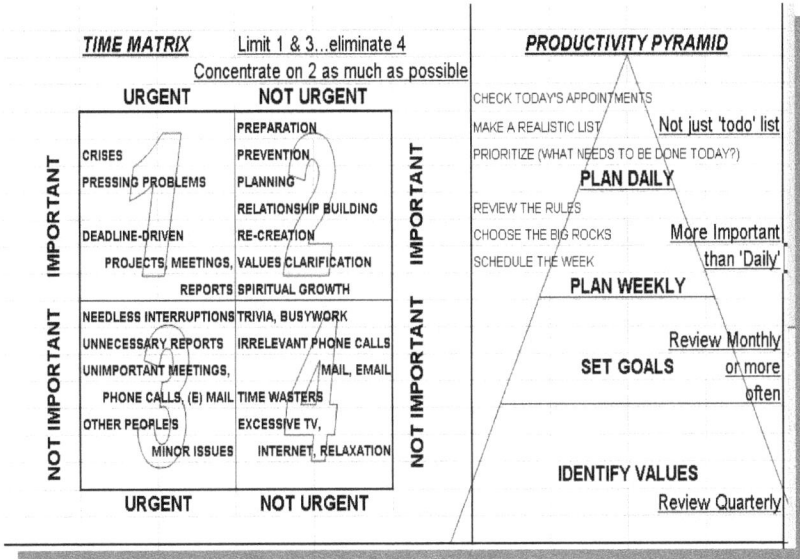

© Charles E.Hummel, InterVarsity Press used by permission

The "Urgent / Important" matrix is taken from Charles Hummel's book, *"The Tyranny of the Urgent"* published by InterVarsity Press. Why have I included it in a book on *"The Love of God"*, you may ask. The answer is simply that knowing and walking in the Love of God is extremely important to your well-being as a Christian and as a resident of Planet Earth. But because we constantly have a 'lifetime' ahead of us, it does not fall into the category of 'urgent'.

Those issues in life that are both 'IMPORTANT' and 'NOT URGENT' are what have the potential to create the most havoc in our lives when left until the 'urgent' stage. So being aware of and heeding the warnings of this matrix is why this simple but critically important appendix is included.

The top left is Quadrant #1. If it is is both <u>Important</u> and <u>Urgent</u> then don't think about it. Better get 'er done.

---

[150] This brief summary of Mr. Hummel's work entitled The Tyranny of the Urgent is critical to any serious life's plan...whether career, family or spiritual. It is presented here to help with the journey. For more help by all means get his book. It is available at a discount through the publisher. Simply email bookstore@axxiom.org.

Quadrant #3 (<u>Urgent</u> / <u>Not Important</u>); if it is not important then the urgency is someone else's. Get these done if you can as time allows.

And Quadrant #4 (<u>Not Urgent</u> and <u>Not Important</u>). These are similar to #3 only less of a priority.

Now, about #2. These are the things in your life that are *Important* but *Not Urgent*.

This is where improving your marriage, planning for the kids' college and spiritual growth all fit (assuming your marriage is fine and your kids are still in grade school).

If you were to skip everything in quadrant #2 for the next few days you know it probably wouldn't matter much. Which is exactly why you need to do something toward accomplishing your quadrant #2 entries at least every week (or more).

<u>These are the things in your life that really hurt if you wait until they're urgent</u>.

So first start with creating a habit of getting into God's Word (and getting God's Word into you)[151] and set about regular work on everything else in that little box.

---

[151] The catch-phrase describing *The OnePage Solution* is *"Bringing the whole world into the Whole Word line never before."* Bible societies, Missionaries and Churches have had great success in bringing the Word to the world. Now what is needed is to bring that world to the Word *like never before*. Get the Word in you. You'll never be the same!

APPENDIX F:

Where Are Your Values?

Once you begin noticing values in yourself you will inevitably notice symptoms of contrasting values in others. Typically this is for your own assessment and not for their correction.   Your values show Most of us don't think about them much however because everyone else we know has exactly the same values. That's why we associate with them. But what if our values were important. What if they affected, even dictated our lifestyle and future. What if our values not only directed (and reflected) our destinies but held us back from the growth and change we all intrinsically seek.

But 'values' are elusive. Like we just saw, they blend into the background because everyone we know is just the same.

So this appendix is designed to be a mirror. We would like to think that our values are as good as anyone else's… just like our theology or our 'goodness' on the *'Hitler-to-Mother-Theresa'* scale.

One writer insightfully pointed out that prejudice and closed-mindedness are very easily discovered, analyzed and diagnosed…in other people.

Shakespeare wrote, "*To thine own self be true."* And Jesus said the same in many ways; the most graphic being, "*And why do you look at the speck in your brother's eye, but do not consider the plank in your own eye?"*

Look at these values and attributes honestly; not for bragging rights or for the sake of criticizing others but for your own spiritual, intellectual, social and even career and economic growth.

Category explanations and 'row' scores:

CATEGORY		VALUES THAT:
Endangering	-20	put lives at risk
Empty	-10	have no substance
Entertaining	0	make you feel good
Enabling	+10	benefit others short term
Enduring	+20	benefit others long term
Eternal	+30	affect eternity

If you really want to see where your values are then (honestly) select the box under each column heading where your values (attitude) most closely fit.

Then use the assigned score for each row to calculate a total. This exercise is designed to give hints as to where our lives need work. It is not a medical or clinical analysis. For that you need a good Christian counselor. So be honest with yourself and see what happens.

The 'Values Chart' is on the next two pages.

The 'unofficial' guide to your total score follows on page 142.

VALUES CATEGORY	ATTRIBUTES	SPIRITUAL	SOCIAL	CONVER-SATION
ENDANGERING (-20)	Drugs, crime, hedonism, unforgiving	I believe God is a myth	Gangs, family	How evil the establishment is
EMPTY (-10)	TV as background noise, lack of direction	I believe in a supreme being	Friends from work, bar, family	Cliches, platitudes, TV shows, problems, anything negative
ENTERTAINING (0)	Magazines, celebrities. sports	I believe God loves me	Anyone who will listen Or with something new to tell	Cars, fashion, guns, scores & statistics, other people, negative
ENABLING (+10)	Education, outreach to the under-privileged, writing	I am God's hands	Academia, anyone upscale	Things, places, politics, people, psy-chology, some-what negative
ENDURING (+20)	Character, integrity, outreach of all kinds, compassion	I believe Jesus loves me	Others that are challenging, honest, real, better than me in some area	Ideas, philosophy, concepts, solutions, mostly positive
ETERNAL (+30)	Word oriented, love, forgiving, compassion, grace, truth	The God of creation purchased my redemption with His blood through Jesus	Friend to all, close with those of like faith, account-ability, anyone better	Faith, eternity, God's Word, Bible solutions, and instruction

BOOKS	PRIORITIES	PASSION	NEWS	ETERNITY
None	Thrill, something for nothing	Get rich	Street	Who cares
TV Guide, magazines, short romance novels	Work, bills, problems, the lottery	None	Headlines, email, internet, magazines	Doesn't exist
Romance novels, Sports Almanac, tell-all exposes	'My team' 'My magazine' 'My show' the lottery	Knowing something new about someone	Fashion or Sports page, tabloids, all broadcast media	If there is a God then I'm sure I'm OK
Texts, reference, research journals, bio-graphies, Bible stories	Reaching out to help others, philanthropic, support noble causes	Problem solving, possibly a hobby or academic cause	Media, journals, upscale publications	I'm doing way better than most people I know
Biographies, novels, research, Bible instruction, inspirational	Living and sharing quality in life, helping others, personal growth	Strong and apparent passion, champion of a single noble cause	Original sources, selected media	As long as I know Jesus I'm OK
Bible, biographies, theology, reference, research, inspiration, devotionals	Knowing, understanding and sharing the Word of God, leading others to Christ, growth	Hearing from God, obeying God, Knowing God better, one single God-given cause	Selected sources, but not always necessary	This life is the shortest span of our eternal existence. I look for His return.

SCORE	SUGGESTION
-100 to -200	Get help / counseling.
-90 to 0	Rethink your time spent thinking and talking about people you don't even know. And know that you have a God-given gift. Consider discovering and sharing that gift with others.
10 to 100	You have begun to realize your God-given potential. Keep searching / growing.
110 to 200	This is about as high as anyone ever attains. A whole new life awaits those who dare strive to grow beyond this level.
210 to 300	Pray about any low points but work on improving and developing your strengths. Never stop growing.

And remember, this is an exercise only and is not intended to diagnose or treat any psychological or pathological or medical condition.

Use of this exercise is simply an indicator of areas that may need attention according to Ephesians 1:17-18. Sound Christian counseling is always a good idea even if things seem to be going smoothly. We can always do better.

Our prayer is that you will continue in God's Word and pursue Spiritual and Personal Growth through your Church, Friends, Family and / or Professional Counseling.

Thanks for being a part of God's Kingdom and pursuing His Truth. Spread the Word!

DISCUSSION
and
ACTION
QUESTIONS

CHAPTER ONE

1.   How do you feel about the description of God's grace? *"God's overwhelming desire to treat you and me as if sin never existed."* Can you even imagine what that would be like?

2.   Describe a time when you found yourself in a position where it was more difficult to receive than to give.

3.   What do you think are our most prominent challenges to receiving the love of God as described in this chapter? How would life look different if could ever comprehend this kind of love?

4.   Read carefully verses 17-23 and tell someone or journal thoroughly your thoughts on each line.

CHAPTER TWO

1.   Verses 4-7 comprise a lofty description of God's love. Meditate on these four verses but tell or journal what you believe the Holy Spirit is saying in verse seven.

2.   Have you been obedient to verses 8-10? Share or write out your testimony.

3.   In chapter two Paul speaks of both the old and the new man as well as the Jew and Gentile...sometimes mixing and blurring the analogies. Pick out a couple of verses and explain if they are clear or raise questions for you.

4.   Discuss the concept presented by the author that the mind is the connection between the flesh and the spirit.

CHAPTER THREE

1.   Read verse ten in the light of God's immeasurable love and talk about what that verse really means.

2.   The author said regarding verses 17-19 that "...if you're ok with that then you haven't got it." Do you agree? Try to explain what the Spirit is saying in these verses.

3.   What would you do differently if you really believed verse 12?

4.   What does it mean to be rooted and grounded in love?

CHAPTER FOUR

1.   Unity is mentioned in the first few verses of chapter four. How would you define the unity that the Holy Spirit is speaking about here through the Apostle? Is He talking about within the local church or among denominations? Or is He as some suggest, speaking to all beliefs and faiths?

2.   Was Adam given authority over the earth? And if he had that authority how was it conveyed to satan? What happened then when Jesus stripped satan of all he had? And finally, considering all this, what is our position of authority / ownership in the earth today? Is it figurative, literal or as some use the term, 'spiritual'?

3.   How do you feel about the author's statement that the 'spiritual' is more real than the 'physical'?

4.   Discuss the author's statement, *"Faith is believing God's promises and Grace is how He delivers those promises to you and me in the natural (physical) realm."*

CHAPTER FIVE

1.   What does it mean to be a follower or 'imitator' of God? Can we as the Amplified Version puts it, *"...imitate God as dear children imitate their parents."* (AMP)

2.   Why are we admonished to *"...be not unwise but understanding what the will of the Lord is"*? And how can we possibly know? Especially if our question regarding His will is not specifically covered in scripture?

3.   Do you agree that submission is a commandment for all the body of Christ and not just for certain relationships? Why?

4.   What are some typical questions that 'gender strife'? And what is your response to them? If you don't know then practice *"...and be ready always to give an answer to every man that asketh you a reason of the hope that is in you with meekness and fear."*
1 Peter 3:15

CHAPTER SIX

1.   How can you be *"...strong in the Lord and in the power of His might"*? A clue is in Hebrews 3:1 and 1 Corinthians 4:13

2.   How is it possible to deal with those who are used of the enemy to come against us at the time of confrontation (according to Ephesians 6:12)? In other words, what do you say to your boss when his criticism is harsh and possibly even unjust?

3.   Why is the shield of faith to be taken 'above all'?

4.   How did Jesus use the 'Sword of the Spirit' in His ministry?

ADDITIONAL SCRIPTURE REFERENCES FOR APPENDIX
'D'

13 But to which of the angels has He ever said:
"Sit at My right hand, Till I make Your enemies Your footstool"?
14 Are they not all ministering spirits sent forth to minister for
those who will inherit salvation?   HEBREWS 1:13-14   (NKJV)

No evil shall befall you, Nor shall any plague come near your
dwelling;11 For He shall give His angels charge over you,
To keep you in all your ways.
12 In their hands they shall bear you up, Lest you dash your
foot against a stone.   PSALM 91:10-12   (NKJV)

Bless the LORD, you His angels,
Who excel in strength, who do His word,
Heeding the voice of His word.   PSALM 103:20   (NKJV)

Set a guard, O LORD, over my mouth;
Keep watch over the door of my lips.   PSALM 141:3 (NKJV)

"Your words have been harsh against Me," Says the LORD,
"Yet you say, 'What have we spoken against You?'
14 You have said, 'It is useless to serve God; What profit is it
that we have kept His ordinance, And that we have walked as
mourners Before the LORD of hosts?
15 So now we call the proud blessed,
For those who do wickedness are raised up;
They even tempt God and go free.'"
16 Then those who feared the LORD spoke to one another,
And the LORD listened and heard them;
So a book of remembrance was written before Him
For those who fear the LORD And who meditate on His name.
                                    MALACHI 3:13-16 (NKJV)

Be anxious for nothing, but in everything by prayer and supplication, with thanksgiving, let your requests be made known to God; 7 and the Peace of God, which surpasses all understanding, will guard your hearts and minds through Christ Jesus. 8 Finally, brethren, whatever things are true, whatever things are noble, whatever things are just, whatever things are pure, whatever things are lovely, whatever things are of good report, if there is any virtue and if there is anything praiseworthy —meditate on these things. 9 The things which you learned and received and heard and saw in me, these do, and the God of Peace will be with you.   PHILIPPIANS 4:6-9 (NKJV)

7 Beloved, let us love one another, for love is of God; and everyone who loves is born of God and knows God. 8 He who does not love does not know God, for God is love. 9 In this the love of God was manifested toward us, that God has sent His only begotten Son into the world, that we might live through Him. 10 In this is love, not that we loved God, but that He loved us and sent His Son to be the propitiation for our sins.
                                        1 JOHN 4:7-10   (NKJV)

Gary lives in Colorado and has four grown children in Oklahoma, California, Texas and Pennsylvania. He also has eight wonderful grandchildren and one (also wonderful) great grand daughter.

Other publications include:
- *Life's Answers for the Over-Committed*[152]
- *Shalom: The Power of Peace*[153]
- *Psalm 119—An English Acrostic*[154]
- *The Gospel of Mark; An Unconventional Commentary*[155]
- *The Ararat Conspiracy*[156]

His passion and calling has always been Teaching, Preaching and studying the Word of God. Aside from this and his writing he has also co-founded the San Luis Valley Christian Center in South Central Colorado.

He can be contacted through the following websites: *TheOnePageSolution.com; TOPS. Axxiom.org; BibleHealing.org; SLVCC.org* or directly at *GJohnson@SLVCC.org*

All publications listed can be previewed and ordered online at www.SLVCC.org.

---

[152] A unique Bible immersion program that ignores chapter divisions and time limits. All the while increasing time in the New Testament to be equal with the Old without skipping a syllable...and constantly including Psalms and Proverbs. Unique is an understatement!

[153] *Shalom,* the Hebrew word for 'peace' goes much deeper than what we call peace. And according to Jesus you can have all that was originally intended.

[154] A never-before published cross cultural printing of this unique passage. Read (and enjoy) like the ancient Hebrews.

[155] The entire volume with footnotes and commentary. A guaranteed eye-opener.

[156] A gripping historical fiction novel out soon.